A DEGREE FOR HENRY

A DEGREE FOR HENRY

STORIES FROM MINNESOTA'S STILLWATER PRISON

CHARLES SLABAUGH

Copyright © 2021 by Charles Whitney Slabaugh, Jr.

Library of Congress Control Number:		2021918468
ISBN:	Hardcover	978-1-6641-9384-0
	Softcover	978-1-6641-9385-7
	eBook	978-1-6641-9386-4

All rights reserved. No part of this book may be reproduced or transmitted in any form or by any means, electronic or mechanical, including photocopying, recording, or by any information storage and retrieval system, without permission in writing from the copyright owner.

Any people depicted in stock imagery provided by Getty Images are models, and such images are being used for illustrative purposes only.
Certain stock imagery © Getty Images.

Print information available on the last page.

Rev. date: 09/10/2021

To order additional copies of this book, contact:
Xlibris
844-714-8691
www.Xlibris.com
Orders@Xlibris.com
833905

CONTENTS

The Cast vii
Glossary ix
Author's Note xiii

Chapter 1   A Nice Day for a Drive in the Country 1
Chapter 2   Infamous Stillwater Prison 10
Chapter 3   E Shop 31
Chapter 4   Literacy 1 37
Chapter 5   Meeting the Group 40
Chapter 6   English Is a Big Problem 68
Chapter 7   Reading Is Fundamental 77
Chapter 8   Doug Has a Bad Day 101
Chapter 9   Mayhem 108
Chapter 10   A New Career Is Born 117
Chapter 11   Not Everyone Fits the Mold 120
Chapter 12   Bad Decision 127
Chapter 13   The Sound of Music 137
Chapter 14   A New Walking Partner 143
Chapter 15   A New Man 150
Chapter 16   New Direction and a New Goal 162
Chapter 17   Disaster 166

Index 175

The Cast

Armstrong, Donte	Inmate woodworker
Bishop, Dale	Lifer inmate, tutor
Blumenthal, Dr. Orland	Stillwater's doctor
Colchran, Bob	Staff, head of "E" shop
Dassel, Pauly	Inmate, tutor, and SO
Dent, Samuel (Sammy)	Inmate, Nathan Osborne's cousin
Diamond, Bernard	Inmate, Lit 1 student
Dombroski, Shirley	Professor, Northfield, Minnesota College
Eckonalanza, Soma	Inmate, student from Ethiopia
Garza, Raphael	Inmate, Lit 1 student
Gilbertson, Sean	Staff, Stillwater chaplain, and Roman Catholic priest
Gravenhorst, Cecil	Inmate, student, tutor, and lifer
Halverson, Jane	Staff, Lit 1 instructor, and head of Literacy at Stillwater
Jacobs, Arturo	Inmate
Jergens, Donald	Inmate, tutor, and head of poetry group
Jiminez, Ernestine	Mother of Henry Jiminez
Jiminez, Henry	Inmate, student, and SO
Johns, Ned	Inmate, lifer
Kline, Steven	Inmate, tutor
Kolkins, Norma	Staff, head of Spector program
Lee, Shoua	Inmate, Hmong student
Marcus, Stanley	Staff, head of testing and higher-education program
Oogolala, Omar	Inmate, student from Sudan, lifer
Osborne, Nathan	Inmate

Polinski, Pamela	Staff, director of Education
Rasmusson, Paul	Inmate, transfer from California system, lifer
Simonton, Ben	Inmate, transfer from Texas system
Sorenson, Douglas	Inmate, tutor, and trained lawyer
Sullivan, Harold	Inmate, tutor
Tofte, Owen	Inmate, swamper
Warren, Robert	Staff, sergeant, D house

Glossary

assignment	any school or job that an inmate is scheduled to attend
bit	inmate slang for how much time a man is serving in prison
C/O	correction's officer
Canteen	prison store where inmates purchase food, candy, hygiene products, clothing, hobby items, and some approved appliances
cho	short for cho-mo
cho-mo	inmate slang for a child molester
contraband	anything an inmate is not allowed to have
controlled movement	the system used at MCF – Stillwater to rigidly control the movement of inmates outside of their assigned cell halls
count	the process where staff verifies that everyone is present.
DOC	Department of Corrections
emergency count	done after weather emergencies or whenever anything unusual has occurred – same as standing count, except each inmate must hold his ID tag and show it two the two C/Os doing the count
gate fee	a system where inmates are forced to saved a portion of their prison earnings so they will have some cash in their pocket when released; Initially, this was set at $100. In the mid-2000s, it was increased to $500, collected at a rate of $100 per year. Half of the inmate's earnings are deducted and placed in this account.
incident report	report generated by staff for almost any, other than ordinary, occurrence inside the prison system

indigent bag	hygiene and other supplies given to men with no money; they contained soap, deodorant, laundry detergent, a comb, writing paper, two no. 10 envelopes and one large manuscript envelope, fifty sheets of plain paper, and a pen; To qualify, an inmate must have no assignment and less than $1 on his books
LOP	loss of privileges
MCF – Faribault	a former state mental hospital converted to be a men's prison in the late 1990s and then rebuilt at substantial expense in the late 2000s; now Minnesota's largest prison
MCF – Red Wing	small prison for juvenile offenders
Minncor	runs all prison industry and the Canteen in Minnesota prison system
Offender	politically-correct term for inmate
SEG	segregation unit
Shank	usually a homemade knife, but it can also be anything an inmate can fabricate to cut or hurt another
Snitch	to report or tell on someone; anyone who does so is then called a snitch
SO	sexual offender
Spector program	a federally-financed program of higher education; named for Pennsylvania senator, Arlen Spector, its sponsor
SRD	scheduled release date
Standing Count	the way count was done at Stillwater; inmates stand anywhere in their cell, facing the door with the overhead light on
State-Issue	approved clothing (jeans, shirts, T-shirts, briefs, socks, and shoes) that each inmate may draw once a year
Swamper	term for a janitor
Switch in	command given requiring all inmates to return to their cell
The Flag	the ground level at Stillwater's living units, so named because they are covered with native flagstone.
The Hole	inmate slang for the segregation unit
UA	short for Unauthorized Area
UA	Urine Analysis test
unauthorized area	any area an inmate is not to enter
violator	an inmate who has failed at parole and is returned to prison

WHEN YOU'VE BEEN PITCHED HEAD FIRST INTO HELL, YOU JUST WRITE ABOUT IT.
—Alexander Solzhenitsyn

Author's Note

On July 19, 2000, I was delivered to Stillwater Prison (Minnesota Correctional Facility – Stillwater) in Bayport, Minnesota. For the next 3,466 days, I lived in that institution until I was transferred to a medium-custody prison on January 14, 2010.

During my years at Stillwater, I met, lived with, and knew several thousand men who found themselves in similar circumstances. In going through that experience with them, I learned a great deal about modern prison life and about myself. This book is about some of those men.

The stories are true. The names are not. Other than mine, everyone's name is fictionalized. To enhance readability, some characters are combined with others. Any mistakes, errors, or omissions are the result of my imperfect memory or my error and are unintentional.

If you have a friend or relative in prison anywhere, please write them a letter or, better yet, arrange to visit them. They will be very pleased to hear from you.

Whit Slabaugh

Bless this prison for having been in my life.
The meaning of earthly existence lies, not as we've grown
accustomed to thinking, but in the development of the soul.
—Alexander Solzhenitsyn

Chapter 1

A Nice Day for a Drive in the Country

It was a beautiful spring morning in June 2000, and the familiar landscape of I-35 in Southern Minnesota flashed by the car window. I eagerly tried to take in every sight and bit of color. I had made this drive countless times – thousands of times – and I knew it by heart. This morning I was desperately trying to see it all and to remember it in perfect detail. My desperation was the product of the knowledge that I would possibly never see these scenes again or at least not for many years. I was riding in the back of a sheriff's car, and that car was transporting me to the Minnesota State Prison in St. Cloud.

Two years before, Lynn, my wife of fifteen years, had been murdered in our home on an equally beautiful spring morning. The intervening twenty-four months had been an often confusing period of depressing accusations and charges, interspersed with periods of hopeful anticipation and even a few brief bolts of optimism. In the end, the optimism proved misplaced, the anticipation turned to depression, and I was convicted after a jury wrestled with the case for two full days. The prosecutor, in his victorious news conference, gloated that he had convicted me despite there being no direct evidence of my guilt. He pointed to his skills in the theater of the courtroom as the reason for the verdict. That morning, as the fields of Southern Minnesota flashed by the car's windows, I was filled with dread and fearful anticipation of what I would find at St. Cloud Prison, MCF – St. Cloud.

My life had been busy and, I thought, productive, but in terms of a criminal record, it had been pretty dull. In the fall of 1998, when I had been arrested, almost one hundred days after Lynn's murder, an officious clerk with the Minnesota

CHARLES SLABAUGH

Department of Corrections, as she interviewed me for a bail hearing, said, "I have your criminal history here. You were convicted for speeding in Eagle Lake in October of 1987."

She was correct; I hadn't been much of a criminal. Now, however, I was a convicted felon and had been sentenced the previous morning to almost thirty years in prison. I was fifty-three years old that day. Under Minnesota's policy, I would be incarcerated until I was seventy-three years old because of Minnesota's system of serving two-thirds of one's sentence in prison and completing the remaining one-third on parole. The numbers didn't seem real to me. I didn't feel fifty-three, but the idea of living to age seventy-three was almost beyond my ability to comprehend. As my mind sorted through the grim reality of my situation, the lush Minnesota farm landscape continued to flash by the speeding car's windows.

We skirted Metropolitan Minneapolis, and in a little over two hours, we were pulling up to the gate of the prison, MCF – St. Cloud. For many years, this old facility had served as a reformatory for wayward youths, but it had recently been converted to an intake facility for the entire state system. I had often viewed the prison's black outer wall from the vantage of Minnesota Highway 10; a four-lane thoroughfare that went from the Twin Cities of Minneapolis and St. Paul, northwest through the state, to Fargo, the gateway to the Dakotas. From the highway, the wall and the buildings looked black and cold. Up close, they looked charcoal and shoddy. As I was to learn, the huge wall and the entire prison had been built by inmate labor almost one hundred years before using granite quarried on the spot. St. Cloud was known as Granite City, and now I was going to live within those uneven walls.

As the steel gate rolled open, the sheriff's car pulled inside, and quickly, I was to begin the intake process. I was stripped, dressed in a coverall, photographed, interviewed, and issued my state issue of clothing (consisting of three pairs of jeans, three blue long-sleeved shirts, six T-shirts, six briefs, six pairs of socks, and one pair of sneakers), fed a cold lunch, and installed in a very austere prison cell. All this occurred in probably less than two hours. Not even the US Army had handled so much bureaucratic pro forma as quickly. As the corrections officer (C/O) was locking me in the cell, he handed me three sheets of paper, telling me that I'd have time to look them over. "Them" turned out to be instructions and information about prison rules and regulations. He was right – I had lots of time. I sat in that cell for the next forty-eight hours with nothing to do but read those sheets and watch out the barred front of the cell. The cell was very dirty, and I cleaned it as best I could using toilet paper. My meals were delivered by an inmate – a cell hall worker, I would later learn. I sat, watched, listened, and thought about my new life. *Welcome to prison*, I thought to myself.

A DEGREE FOR HENRY

I later learned that this initial forty-eight hours of solitary time was part of a period of mandated "quarantine" for all new arrivals at MCF – St. Cloud. The intent was to see how each man responded to the time alone in a bare cell. Apparently, I did all right because at the end of the period, I was allowed to go to the mess hall for meals. I also began my formal orientation.

After that first mess hall meal, I was moved from the quarantine area to a similar cell, high up in the building. The new cell was very dirty, and I spent the afternoon and almost two rolls of single-ply toilet paper trying to clean it up a bit.

During the next five weeks, I attended classes in safety and took several standardized educational tests. All the classes and testing consumed maybe fifteen hours, but they were spread over the next five weeks. The safety classes were very basic, emphasizing the need to read the labels for the various cleaning products that were available to use inside the prison. Each product came in a distinct color, and all were supplied in see-through spray bottles. Each product's label explained how the product was to be used and in what kind of situation. The labels also provided information about what to do if the product was ingested or splashed into the eye.

I noticed that the products were made by Minncor Industries. I would later learn that Minncor was a creation of the Minnesota Legislature and ran all businesses within the Minnesota Department of Corrections. Several years later, Minncor even took over the Canteen system. This was a name I would come to know very well in the years to come.

Classes were taught by an older C/O with a pleasant personality. They reminded me a great deal of the US Army basic training classes. The C/O moved over the material very slowly. Often he would tell us, "You need to remember this." Or "You will see this again."

His obvious tip off as to what materials was going to show up in the coming test seemed completely missed by many in the group. He continued to give that advice, undismayed by our lack of understanding or appreciation. It would have been comical if it had not been so sad.

Although I spent most of my time alone, locked in the five-by-nine cell, on those welcome occasions when I had to attend class, I was usually with the same guys. There was a somewhat confused young black man who kept telling us that he was a teacher, the very quiet middle-aged Mexican who seemed to understand little of what was said, a very young white kid with extremely intense eyes and a very angry way about him, and a young Native who was rumored to have killed his father. They were the ones I remember best of a group that numbered about fifteen men. We would all go to wherever the class was being held, pick seats, and then sit through the meeting or class. When it ended, we would then return to our cells and resume waiting for the next class, meeting, or meal. For one who was used to lots of activity and a very busy personal and business schedule, it was a very slow, difficult, and long five-week ordeal.

Only a few things stick out in my memory from my time at MCF – St. Cloud, but a fight I witnessed the first day specifically stands out in my mind. I was initially housed in quarantine on the second tier of an old building. Actually, all of St. Cloud's buildings looked old, but this one was particularly ugly with cracked mortar and broken bricks visible on its exterior. From my cell, I could look down to the main floor where a number of square tables sat, each with four stools, one attached on each side.

I had been in the cell for only a few minutes, or so it seemed to me, when a loud horn sounded. Almost immediately, I heard steel doors opening and inmates emerging from the cells below me. They quickly sat at the tables, filling every seat. Cards emerged from pockets, and games quickly got underway.

After maybe fifteen minutes, two men at one table began to argue. I wasn't paying a lot of attention at the beginning, but it seemed that they were arguing over what had been bid and then actually made in a game of spades that they were playing. Suddenly, one man reached across the table and slugged his opponent in the face. Quickly, they were both on top of the table. They then rolled onto the floor. There was a splash of blood on one man's shirt, and everyone in the room was yelling. Whistles began to sound, and several C/Os ran into the area, shouting, "Stop that!" and "Switch in!" over and over. The PA system began to sputter, "Switch in! Switch in!"

It repeated over and over. The two men continued to fight, and the crowd continued to yell as they moved toward the cell doors. Then a C/O with sergeant's stripes arrived. He immediately took an aerosol canister from his belt and sprayed something in to the faces of the two men who were still fighting. They immediately stopped fighting and began to gag and rub their eyes. The man on top vomited on the man under him.

Within very few seconds, both men were in handcuffs, and the C/Os began to force the remainder of the crowd back into their cells, under my feet. With a great deal of grumbling and mumbling, the men retreated to their cells and shut their doors. Within a few more minutes, the unit was quiet – very quiet – and only the pungent odor of the spray used by the sergeant lingering in the air offered any proof of the

A DEGREE FOR HENRY

chaos I had just witnessed. I was amazed at the intensity of the brawl and with the quickness of its resolution. No one, C/Os or inmates, seemed surprised or overly upset over what had happened or how quickly things had returned to normal. As I would come to know, normal was an elusive term in prison.

The next few days were a blur of inactivity for me. We went to three meals every day. The food was okay, and there was enough of it, but we were given very little time to eat it. We learned when we came out of the serving line with our tray, to sit down very quickly and to eat quickly. If you didn't eat quickly, you found yourself with food on your tray when the C/Os announced that it was time to go. In that case, the remaining food had to be dumped in a garbage can. With the C/Os announcement, you were finished eating, regardless of what remained uneaten on your tray or how hungry you were.

The weather was beautiful. Minnesota summers are very nice, and we were having bright, warm, sunny June and July days, but we seldom got outside. Three or four times a week we were allowed outside to the yard for less than an hour. Many men played sports, such as basketball, handball, soccer, or touch football. I usually walked laps on the track. During these weeks, we also attended the classes on safety, and we were also tested for reading and math skills.

One day we went to a class where a very old man discussed sexual behavior. He did his best to spell out how we could masturbate in our cell without falling prey to the many C/Os who were constantly patrolling the halls and peering into each man's cell as they passed by. The rule, as he explained it, was to have a sheet or a blanket covering your exposed skin. "If the officer can see skin or your private parts, you are in trouble," was his message.

That day he also asked for volunteers for AIDs testing, but no one took him up on his offer.

All the time at MCF – St. Cloud was an assortment of very long days with almost nothing to do. Being a lifelong reader, I eagerly searched the cellblock's book cart – a small bookcase on wheels usually found near the unit's entrance and exit – to small avail. Many of the books were damaged with pages torn out, and many were science fiction, which had little appeal to me. A book by Prison Fellowship's Charles Colson was of some interest and occupied me for a day. A huge work by Doris Kerns Goodwin about the Kennedys and the Fitzgeralds of Massachusetts fame was a delight and kept me happily engrossed for several days and nights. When my *Time* magazine subscription caught up with me from my former life, it was a cause for rejoicing. Already, I was learning how important small pleasures were to be in this new life.

5

CHARLES SLABAUGH

We were always in a hurry at MCF – St. Cloud with the staff rushing us out of the room while some were still eating, but the Fourth of July meal of 2000 was memorable for me. The menu had been published in advance, and it was substantial: a hamburger, a bratwurst, a quarter of barbequed chicken, potato salad, relish, watermelon, pie, and ice cream. We were all eager for the evening meal, and we were pleased when we were called early for it at 3:30 PM.

Our trip through the line was enticing as our trays were literally heaped with food. We quickly took our seats and dug in. In what seemed like seconds and, in reality, were no more than five minutes, the announcement was made: "Okay, that's it. Dump your trays and head back to the unit."

When I first heard the announcement, I thought it was maybe someone's poor attempt at a joke, but it was not. The staff was demanding that we throw away huge uneaten portions of this special holiday meal. One young man tried to argue. He was quickly in handcuffs and on his way to segregation. Seeing that, the rest of us stuffed what we could in our mouths and headed for the garbage cans.

We later learned the reason for this unfriendly action. Once we were all secured in our cells, the prison went on lockdown and substantial portions of the staff were sent home early for the night. July 4, 2000, was not going to be a happy memory for any of us, but those staff members would get some family time on the holiday.

On Wednesday morning of my fifth week at MCF – St. Cloud, I was paged to the desk in the midmorning. This was unusual, and I had no idea why. My case worker, an agreeable fellow named Wilson, was waiting there for me. "Your PEP meeting is in a few minutes," he announced.

I asked what a PEP meeting was, and he explained that this meeting would be very important as it would set in place the plan for my time in prison. I asked what PEP stood for, and he couldn't remember. He assured me that it was about planning my programming and that it was important. At that, we walked into a room adjoining the cell hall, where three beefy middle-aged men were waiting, seated at a table piled high with folders. There was a chair facing their table, and Wilson motioned for me to take that chair. As I sat down, the middle man in the trio began to talk. He explained that they were my PEP committee. They had examined my case and were prepared to decide my programming. Since arriving at MCF – St. Cloud, I had been told that I would remain there for about forty-five days for orientation. Today he said that I would remain at MCF – St. Cloud for "seven to eight months because Stillwater and Rush City were completely full." Rush City was a brand new prison that was just opening. I had read about it in the newspapers, and MCF – St. Cloud was full of notices, asking inmates to volunteer to go there for good-paying jobs. I was sure that at least part of what he was saying was untrue, but I said nothing. From the time I had arrived at MCF – St. Cloud, I had been told several times that I would remain there for about forty-five days. Obviously, something had changed, but again, I said nothing.

He continued on, asking me about drug use. I answered that I had never done drugs. "But you were in Vietnam," another of the trio interjected.

That was true, but I pointed out that over 8 million Americans had served in Vietnam and not all of us did drugs. The third member of the troika then spoke. "How about alcohol?"

I replied that I had used a great deal of alcohol many years earlier but had handled quitting myself.

"Did you take treatment?" he asked.

I answered, "No, I just quit drinking. I haven't had a drink in about fourteen years."

He had no comment.

After about three minutes, the middle guy said, "Okay, that's it. You will receive a copy of our report."

I asked, "May I say something?" He nodded yes, and I continued, "For five weeks, I've been here with almost nothing to do. Now you're telling me that I'm going to be here for many more months. If that's the case, I urgently need something to do. I've been busy all my life, and this inactivity is very hard on me. I need a job."

With that, the middle guy of the trio said, "Well, we don't have any *good* jobs right now." As he spoke, he gave emphasis to the word "good," and he smirked.

I replied, "Well, if you don't have any good jobs, please give me a bad job."

Instantly, the middle guy jumped to his feet and said, "Are you trying to be a smart ass?"

I said, "No, I'm trying to tell you that I need something to do. Sitting here day after day has been very hard. I urgently need a job."

No one said anything more. Wilson indicated that I should walk with him out of the room. When back in the cell hall, he told me to return to my cell.

About an hour later, I was again paged to the front desk. The C/O on duty said, "Congratulations, you have been hired by the license plant upper. You will be moving to 'A' house. Go pack your property, put it on a cart, and wheel it up here."

I did that, and in fifteen minutes, I was in my new cell in cellblock A. My new cell was identical to my old cell, except that it was dirtier. Using bunches of toilet paper; I cleaned it up as much as possible. I was only somewhat successful in my attempt at cleaning because there were no tools or cleaning supplies available to us.

The next morning I was ready for work right after breakfast, but it was announced that the license plant, upper and lower, were "laid in" for the day – no work. The same thing happened the next day. But the following Monday, I actually went to work. Work consisted of putting new license plates in clear polyester bags and then packing the plates into boxes for shipment to various counties around Minnesota. It certainly wasn't very exciting or challenging, but the five men on the crew were friendly enough, and I was doing something. We talked a bit, and it sure beat lying on my bunk all day with nothing to do. The second day was a repeat of the first. I got to know one man on the crew a bit more, and the day passed quickly. As I walked into cell block "A" after work Tuesday, I heard my name being called – paging me to the front desk. When I got there, I was handed a red version of the gray plastic bins that we stored our property and clothing in. As the C/O handed me the bin, he said, "You are going to Stillwater Friday. Tomorrow you will turn in all your property in this bin."

These bins were about 40 x 24 inches and 18 inches deep. We stored all our property – clothing, hygiene products, medications, food, or snacks in there. We were allowed two bins for everything. I asked, "What about my new job?"

"It's over," he replied. "You're going to Stillwater."

That pretty much confirmed that everything the troika had told me the week before was a lie.

I took the red bin back to my cell and found that the mail had arrived and was lying on the cell floor. In the middle of the pile was my copy of the PEP committee report. In reading the report, I found that the troika had mandated me for chemical and alcohol dependency treatment. I could only conclude that the members of the committee had not believed anything I had told them. I was learning about this new world – nothing that you say was believed or taken at face value. For someone who takes himself fairly seriously, this being incarcerated was going to take some getting used to.

Later I learned that everyone going through MCF – St. Cloud that summer was mandated for chemical and alcohol dependency treatment. This prison program was 100 percent reimbursed by the federal government.

Friday morning, right after breakfast, I was sent to a part of the prison I had never seen before. With eight other men, I was given an orange jumpsuit to wear over my clothing. We were then handcuffed, and a chain was run through our handcuffs, then through a stamped hollow box at our waist, and then down to our ankles, which were secured with manacles. This substantially hobbled us. We could waddle, but running was completely out of the question. Once everyone was dressed and chained up, we were led outside and put in a stretch Ford window van. Every seat in the back was filled. In front, two C/Os (one lieutenant and one corporal) got into van with the lieutenant assuming the driver's seat. We were soon off on the journey to MCF – Stillwater, Bayport, Minnesota.

Chapter 2

Infamous Stillwater Prison

In less than two hours, I saw the light brown walls of Stillwater Prison (MCF – Stillwater, as it is now known). Stillwater would be my home for almost ten years, but that is a long story to follow. Before we could get into Stillwater Prison, the van had to be searched. The lieutenant slowly drove past the huge steel door, which had slipped open on rollers. That door rolled shut behind us, and a similar door to our front closed. As we sat in the van, two C/Os ran mirrors under the van. The hood opened, and the engine compartment was searched. *Do they really think anyone would sneak in?* I thought to myself.

Ultimately, we got inside and were allowed to exit the van. We had to climb an old crumbling set of cement steps. No mean feat with our ankles chained! We entered a large room dominated by a large steel cage.

A young female C/O helped us out of our chains one at a time and directed us into the cage. We sat on benches that lined the cage's perimeter. Some of us utilized the toilet in the rear corner. The toilet was partially shielded from the C/O's view, to the extent that when one sat on the commode, you were visible from your mid-chest upward. What you were doing back there was obvious, but your lower body was not visible as you used the facility. Privacy concerns in prison were always secondary to the overriding, all-consuming need for security.

Soon a C/O approached the cage with a large cardboard box. From the box, he pulled out transparent bags. He passed one to each of us. Each bag contained four slices of bread, several slices of bologna, a container of ketchup and one of yellow mustard, an orange, and one carton of 2 percent milk. Lunch was served. It was quickly consumed.

A DEGREE FOR HENRY

As we finished eating, an older man in a white coat arrived and began calling each of us out by name and OID number. When my name was finally called, I joined the man at a small table for what developed to be a medical interview. The gentleman was a registered nurse, and he had a file on me in front of him. I confirmed that I was hypertensive but that the condition was well controlled with medication. Other than that, my health was pretty good. The conversation took less than five minutes.

I moved on to a meeting with the Property Department. In another brief meeting, I learned that I would not receive my property for several days as the Property Department had to search it, and it was Friday afternoon. I had been in the same clothes for two days already, and this meant I would be in them for at least three more days. I wasn't surprised. My five weeks in prison had already shown me that things like basic hygiene and clean shorts were not important to the operation of the prison's system.

Soon a C/O wearing the insignia of a sergeant arrived and called several names from a list on a clipboard. Mine was the second name he called, so I knew that I was going somewhere. We left the laundry unit where we had been interviewed. We made a hard turn to the left into a big corridor and walked down a huge hall that connected all the sections of the Stillwater Prison. We stopped at a door marked "D Hall." After each of us passed through a metal detector, we entered the unit. Compared to MCF – St. Cloud, the building was huge and tall. I counted five tiers, and the cellblock was double-sided. I would learn that about two hundred inmates (offenders, to the politically-correct) lived in cell hall D. They were supervised by five C/Os on each watch.

Inside the unit, I was quickly assigned a cell on the fifth tier, west side of the building. As I climbed the steps with my bedding in hand, I quickly became aware of just how warm (hot) these old buildings could be in July. Most of Stillwater's buildings were built around 1915. Cell hall D was built in the 1930s. It was the newest of the major housing units.

As I climbed the stairs, the building was quiet and mostly empty as most of the men were away at their jobs. A few inmates moved across the ground floor, which I would soon learn was called the flag. I would later learn that The Flag referred to the ground-floor level covering in all of Stillwater's cellblocks, which was large squares of native flagstone. Some men were using several exercise machines spread around the flag, and others were on a few of the wall-mounted telephones that were clustered near the main desk. There were also several microwaves in the unit, and they got a lot of use. There were really few men visible in this large building at that time of day. I would soon learn that the west side of D hall housed men working in Stillwater's Minncor Metal Industries, and they were still at work. The east side of D hall was reserved for men working in the kitchen. They worked staggered shifts, covering the kitchen's workday from 4:30 AM to 6:30 PM, seven days a week. Some of them were always in the unit, but they kept mostly to the east side of the building.

The metal shop workers worked in those shops from about 7:15 AM until about 3:15 PM, with a midday break for lunch and the ever-so-important noon count. They went directly from work to lunch. From there, they went to their individual cell. They were locked into those cells so that two C/Os could walk the building's ten tiers and count each man. During count, each man had to be standing in his cell with the overhead light turned on. Having them stand on their feet ensured that each man was breathing, and the light made it easy for the C/Os to identify each man as they passed the door. Upon arrival at MCF – Stillwater, every man received a soft rubbery strip with his name and OID number of the front with a magnetized back. That strip was affixed to flat plate on each cell's door so that everyone knew precisely who belonged in each cell.

The OID number, to the Department of Corrections, was more important than the man's name. Assigned during the intake process, the six-digit number was embossed on each man's plastic ID tag that every inmate wore on his shirt. With a picture above the OID number, that tag easily identified each of us. We wore that tag whenever we left the unit.

We used the OID number at all times with our name. Incoming mail had to include that number or the mail was returned to the sender as "undeliverable." If a man was released from prison and then came back to prison years later with a new charge, he still had the same number. When I arrived in the summer of 2000, the DOC was assigning numbers beginning with 20. From a man's number, we could roughly tell when he had first encountered the system.

As I did not have a job, I was quickly locked in my cell. High up on the fifth tier, I was sweating. The sides of cell hall D were lined with high windows that were open in the heat of July. I remember how dirty all those windows were.

The cell I was in was dirty too. It contained a steel bunk, constructed of angle iron frames with a steel sheet for a deck. On the deck sat a foam mattress that I estimated at 5 inches in thickness. The mattress was lumpy. Mounted on the other side of the cell was a one-piece steel desk and wardrobe unit. A toilet was in a corner of the back of the cell with a sink in the middle. A small plastic mirror hung above the sink. It was scratched and cloudy and revealed a weak image when I looked in it.

A DEGREE FOR HENRY

I set about to make my bed and get my few possessions in order. I would learn that "property" was the prison term for what little I still owned. The cell was pretty bare but did contain two new rolls of single-ply toilet tissue. I used most of one roll in a somewhat futile attempt to clean the desk, sink, and toilet in the cell. It seemed that all of the cell's flat surfaces were very dirty, and so was the cell's cement floor.

Shortly after 3:00 PM, the noise level in the unit picked up as most of the residents who worked in the metal shops returned from work. As they filtered onto the tiers and into their individual cells, they talked, joked, and were obviously glad that their workweek was over. Conversations ranged from weekend plans to how the Twins were going to fair in the current series with New York's Yankees. The mood was light and cheerful. For the most part, they ignored me. I was just some new guy, locked in his cell, as they went about the routine of ending the workweek.

As I watched them, I was struck by the contrast from my assumptions of what Stillwater's inmates would be like and the reality before me. After all, Stillwater is a "close custody" facility. With the exception of the supermax facility at nearby Oak Park Heights, this was the highest level of security Minnesota ran; a very serious place filled with very determined, often dangerous men. Now I was one of them.

These men seemed almost *normal*. True, many sported lots of tattoos, and there was a huge variety of haircuts, beard and mustache combinations, but no one really looked sinister or menacing. As a group, they looked dirty, but I assumed that came from their work in Stillwater's Metal Industries building. These men made steel school desks, heavy farm equipment, and snow plow blades for the Minnesota Department of Transportation. They bent, cut, and shaped metal; all of it dirty, hard work. As if on cue, many of them grabbed soap and towels and headed for the showers on the flag level. For the most part, they looked just like factory workers everywhere, anxious to wash away the job's soil and get on with the rest of the day.

The PA system suddenly blared my name and also the names of the three other new men in the unit, telling us to report to the front desk. Locking my cell behind me, I quickly headed down to the desk where an older sergeant was waiting for us. He explained that he was the second-watch D hall sergeant. He told us that we would not be receiving our property for several days as it was Friday afternoon, and he offered to take us down to the Property Department where we could get some clean used socks, underwear, or whatever to tide us over. One young fellow said that he didn't want anyone's used underwear and asked why he couldn't get new stuff. The sergeant quickly shot down that idea, but the other new guy and I

CHARLES SLABAUGH

quickly joined the sergeant on a trip to the Property Department, which was just closing for the day. Inside the Property Department, we were directed to several bins of clean usable clothing, to which we helped ourselves.

As it turned out, we were not called to Property to claim our clothing until the following Tuesday afternoon. We were both grateful to the sergeant for his thoughtful offer.

About 4:10 PM, I began to hear many steel doors slamming shut, and soon a loud gong sounded. From my experience at MCF – St. Cloud, I assumed that we were heading into the afternoon count. Count was a big deal at MCF – St. Cloud, and I assumed it would be here too.

The count ritual consumed about thirty minutes. Without announcement, about 4:50 PM, everyone's cell door made a clicking noise and unlocked – my door included. At first, I was surprised, and then I remembered that as a TU (temporarily-unemployed Inmate), I could be out of my cell in the evenings. Immediately, the noise level in the building began to rise, and the catwalk on the tier began to fill with men.

Most of them continued to ignore me. A few nodded or said "hi," but I was an unknown, a new guy. The old hands knew that I wouldn't be around long. Once I found a job, I would be moved to another unit.

In twenty more minutes, a one word announcement came over the PA system: "Chow."

Everyone began moving to the stairs, heading down to the unit's exit to the main hall and supper. I joined the line. The meal was grilled cheese sandwiches (two!), a bowl of tomato soup, french fries, with an apple for desert. The sandwiches were cold with hard stale bread crusts, and the fries were soggy, but I was hungry and ate all of it. Unlike St. Cloud, we had plenty of time to eat the meal. In Stillwater's controlled-movement system, a unit came to supper as a group. We came as a group, we ate as a group, and we had to return to our unit as a group. When we finished eating, we all sat until the red light in the front of the dining room turned green. When that light changed, it was our signal to get up, head to the exit, and return to D hall.

The dining room could seat about five hundred men, but it was split right down the middle by a cement block wall, maybe 8 feet tall. To enter the room, we used one of four cafeteria-style serving lines and were routed to the east portion of the divided room or to the west side. Today we were on the east side. As we filed in and took seats at the many square four-man tables in the east room, another unit was already eating their supper in the west room. Once we were all served and seated in the east room, the light in the west room turned from red to green. Without a word, that unit got out of their seats, filed out, and returned to their unit while we began to eat. Once that first unit was all back inside their living unit and the door was secured, another unit would be called to the mess hall. They would walk to the mess hall, collect their meals, and fill the west room. There were never more than two of Stillwater's six units out of their cell halls at the same time. Controlled movement was a way of life at MCF – Stillwater.

As I was to later learn, controlled movement was the key to the overall security system at Stillwater. All men who worked in a specific job lived in the same living unit. When it came time for them to go to work, the command was issued for a specific job to "switch out" to work. While they were on their way to work, they were the only inmates outside of their living unit or assigned job. It worked the same way for movement to the gym, the yard, or the courtyard. The intent was to ensure that only those with a specific reason to be out of a controlled room were actually out.

If an individual had to go somewhere – to the health services, to the Property Department, for example – that inmate would be given a computer-generated pass embossed with his name and OID number. He had ten minutes to arrive and check in at his destination. In another time, inmates roamed the complex more or less at will, but those days were long gone at Stillwater. It was a well-planned system of keeping the prison under control at all times, and it worked.

The meal consumed most of my attention. I was hungry, and the menu had sounded good. The soup was the best part of the meal. It was hot and rich with bits of vegetables mixed in. I used it to dunk the cold hard-crusted sandwiches in and found that made the meal okay. I enjoyed the delicious small red apple too, although I noticed that many of the men did not eat theirs. Some left the apple on their tray, which they took to a larger table with a hole in the center when they finished their meal. At that table, an inmate worker sat with a scraper in his hand. He took each man's tray and scrapped the remnants of the meal into the table's center hole, which had a large garbage can under it.

A few men left their apples on the dining table, but many attempted to trade them for food that other men didn't want to eat. The most frequent offer was to attempt to trade an apple for fries. Few of that trade were actually completed, but you had to admire the attempt, I figured. I could see that french fries, even soggy ones, were highly-prized items at Stillwater, while apples were not.

CHARLES SLABAUGH

After what seemed like a long, long wait, the unit that had been going through the serving lines while we ate was finally all seated in the west room. Our light turned green from red. Immediately, D hall rose to its feet and headed for the door.

Back inside D hall, some men made a dash for the washing machines. There were two washers and two electric driers on each side of the building. All were Maytag brand commercial machines and looked to be in good order and repair. This was good news. At MCF – St. Cloud, our laundry was done for us. We sent our laundry out in a securely-tied bag. The Laundry Department washed and dried it all still inside the bag. It was returned to us a tangled mess, often still damp. Doing the laundry ourselves would be a great improvement, although, as I was to learn, having only four machines for two hundred men presented more than a few problems in finding available machines.

Other men headed for a telephone or to one of the living unit's many exercise machines. Others gathered at the several six-man card tables to play various card or board games. Very quickly, D hall was a very busy place.

I walked around, exploring my new home. On a bulletin board near the main desk, I noticed a posted memo dated the previous Thursday, listing all the available inmate job openings at Stillwater. A note at the bottom of this posting advised that anyone interested in a job opening should complete a green job application and place it in the outgoing mailbox by Sunday evening.

Very much interested in getting a job, I approached the staff desk and asked where to find the required green application forms. A not unfriendly C/O pointed to a sheet of green paper hanging from a slot of the front of the desk. He told me to make a separate application for each job I was interested in. I took several forms and spent the rest of the evening in my cell completing application forms. I applied for every job listed, regardless of whether I had the required qualifications or not. I really wanted a job.

Several of the jobs called for specific experience or skills I did not have: "Welding" and "experienced electricians" were two skills I knew I wasn't qualified for, but I made my application anyway. My vivid memory of the weeks in MCF – St. Cloud, passing each day on my bunk, was clearly on my mind.

Prison jobs did not pay well, but those with jobs had many more privileges than those without jobs. They were allowed to be out of their cells must more often than were unemployed men, and I already knew how little there was to do in prison.

16

For jobs classed as state support, the kitchen and cell hall swamper's jobs, the pay began at 25¢ an hour and could rise to $1 an hour. Minncor jobs started at 50¢ an hour and could go up to $2 an hour. In both categories, one was eligible for a 25¢ an hour raise every ninety days. Jobs as students in education paid a flat rate of 50¢ an hour. Tutor jobs in education ran from 50¢ to $1 an hour. The tutor rate was later raised to $1.50 an hour. As I reflected on this pay scale, I remembered my first job as a part-time stock boy at a local department store started at $1 per hour in 1962. We sure weren't keeping up with inflation!

Life world be a bit more pleasant at Stillwater as I would be allowed to purchase a TV and a radio. Even with those much-sought-after essentials of modern life, I knew that being locked in a six-by-nine cement-lined cell made for very long days and nights. Indeed, I very much wanted a job - any job.

At about 8:00 PM, the PA system announced, "Final pill run," and it occurred to me that I had not yet received my medications. I took several medications daily for hypertension, and those medications had been taken from me at MCF – St. Cloud before I left for Stillwater. The C/O who had taken them had assured me that I would get them when I arrived at MCF – Stillwater. The PA announcement had reminded me that I had not gotten them back.

I immediately left my cell and went to the main D hall staff desk, by the front door. An older sergeant was standing at the desk, speaking on the phone, when I got there. I waited for him to finish his call. When he hung up the receiver, he looked at me and said, "Yes."

I quickly explained my dilemma. Without making any comment to me, he picked up the phone and dialed a number from memory. "This is Warren in dog house. I have a transfer from St. Cloud today, Slabaugh," as he read my ID tag, "205155. He has meds that he needs, and you didn't return them to him. I want a callback in two minutes, telling me where they are." With that, he hung up the phone. Looking at me, he said, "Stay right here, this won't take long." With that, the phone rang, and he answered, "Dog house, this is Warren." Then he said, "Okay, we're coming now," and he hung up.

Motioning to me to follow him, we left D house and walked back to the laundry area, where I had arrived earlier in the day. As we entered the laundry, a young C/O ran over to the sergeant with a package of meds. He said, "Sorry, Sergeant, we've had a lot going on today."

Sergeant Warren took the package and handed it to me. "Is that all of them?" he asked, and I confirmed that they were mine and that they were complete.

CHARLES SLABAUGH

He then nodded to the young C/O, and then he and I retraced our steps back to D house. On the way, I said, "Thanks for your help, Sergeant."

Without looking at me, he said, "You don't have to thank me for doing my job."

That was how I came to know Sergeant Warren. I would later learn that he was a legend at Stillwater. He had long run the third watch, 2:00 PM-10:00 PM, at D hall. If you broke the rules, he could be an awful adversary, but if you followed the rules, he would be a good friend. The rumor was that he had years ago declined the chance to advance to the rank of lieutenant, preferring to stay a sergeant and run the unit he knew very well.

On Saturday morning, after a breakfast of cornbread, swimming in sugary syrup, I set out to continue my exploration tour of D house. Even early on Saturday, it was a busy place with men filling the game tables, all the phones were busy, and groups clustered around the exercise machines. I joined a fairly long line of inmates trying to do their laundry after borrowing some Tide detergent from a guy I knew from St. Cloud. He agreed to the loan somewhat reluctantly, but my promise to repay twice the borrowed amount on Canteen day secured the loan.

I soon learned that patience was the key to success in doing one's wash, at least at midday on Saturday. I also learned that almost everyone washed their blue jeans with their white T-shirts, shorts, and socks together. This explained why most everyone's whites were gray. This made sense as the line for a machine was long, and detergent was expensive, so lumping everything together into one large load helped stretch detergent and the money needed to purchase it. I noticed the same man using dishwashing liquid to launder his clothes. I later learned that this was a fairly common thing because dishwashing liquid was much cheaper on the Canteen's price list than was the Tide detergent that everyone preferred.

As I thought about how dirty the metal shop workers got their clothes and how they washed it all without bleach (bleach was absolutely prohibited as it would quickly be used in the prison's illegal-but-always-flourishing tattoo business), it wasn't surprising that everyone's T-shirts quickly took on a medium gray color with lots of stains for accents.

Few inmates had much money. Prison jobs didn't pay much with most jobs beginning at $0.25 per hour. Compounding the low hourly rate of pay, many men were paying fines and/or court-ordered restitution orders or were trying to accumulate the required $100 gate fee savings. To meet those obligations, one half of everything they earned was deducted from their pay. The only bright light in their income situation was that they were exempt from federal or Minnesota income taxes. Prison wages were not income; they were an allowance. I saw more than a few men trying to borrow just enough coffee to make one cup. While I never had been rich, my life had gone pretty well – at least up to this point! – and I had wanted for little. To see men trying to beg or borrow a single cup of coffee reminded me of my early time in the US Army.

Like the army, prison had men without money and those who had money. Again, like the army, prison had those who seemed ready to profit from those without. Some things never seem to change. I had learned in St. Cloud that if you borrowed an item costing $1 this week, you were expected to repay $2 the next week. In some cases, you might be able to make a deal to repay $1.50, but that was a very good deal. The terms depended on who you dealt with and your reputation for repayment. No one challenged the harsh arithmetic and a robust of completely-illegal loan business existed at St. Cloud and Stillwater, where those with more took advantage of those with less.

Men loaned just about everything imaginable, with the C/Os turning a blind eye to most of this activity. Department of Corrections (DOC) rules specifically prohibited any transfer of property between inmates ("No. 190 – No offender shall steal, control, or have in his or her possession any unauthorized property," 2005 Offender Regulations), but Stillwater's staff had lots to do, with several fights occurring daily, the control of drug and alcohol abuse a priority, and outright extortion an ongoing problem; so a guy handing his buddy a package of Kool-Aid merited little attention.

I spent Saturday and Sunday trying to learn as much as I could about my new home. I learned that the policy called controlled movement governed everything at Stillwater. To eat a meal, go to the yard or even the gym; or even to report to your job required that you wait until your group was called for movement to the specified activity. When that movement order was announced (called), the entire group had five minutes to complete the movement. At the end of the five minutes allocated for the movement, another announcement was made: "D house door is closing for _____," and that was it. If you missed the movement for lunch, for example, your next chance to visit the dining room would be the movement for supper. When the supper call was made, you again had five minutes to make that movement, or you wouldn't get another chance to eat that day. We went just about everywhere in a group, with our living unit, or we didn't go at all.

Over that weekend, I visited the yard and the gym several times. I discovered the yard had a walking/running track of almost a quarter of a mile in length and that our periods in the yard were about forty-five minutes, far less than I would have preferred, but to give each living unit a period of their own, excluding count and

CHARLES SLABAUGH

meal times, didn't allow for more. I was disappointed to learn that our library was never open on weekends. To visit the library or chapel, we had to sign up several days in advance. On Sunday, I wanted to attend church services, but I had missed the sign-up the previous week, so I couldn't make that movement.

On that weekend, I frequently heard men paged by name and told to "Report to shakedown." I finally learned that "shakedown" was the gateway to the visiting room. Without exception, men were delighted to hear that call and quickly changed into their best and cleanest clothes before hurrying to the shakedown room. Visits were a very big deal at Stillwater, and I never saw anyone turn one down.

To qualify to receive visits, inmates had to mail a visiting privilege application form to their prospective visitor. The visitor had to complete and sign the form and then mail it back to the prison. At the prison, when the form was reviewed and approved, the inmate was informed that his visiting list had been expanded. It was then up to the inmate to advise the visiting applicant that they had been approved. The inmate also had to inform them of any and all rules and the time that visiting was open. Visits were from one to two hours, Wednesday through Sunday. Each inmate was allowed sixteen approved visitors (later expanded to twenty-four visitors) and sixteen hours of visits per month.

Between trips to the yard and the gym, I saw quite a bit of Stillwater that weekend. I spent some of my time on the flag doing my laundry and just watching activity. The flag was a busy place on the weekend and on weekday evenings. It contained several different exercise/weight-training machines, the washers and dryers, the telephones, a barbershop, and many six-man card/game tables, plus the main staff desk next to the main entrance.

Whenever the flag was open, there were always several card games in progress, some poker, with "Texas Hold 'Em" being the most popular version of the game, but more men seemed to prefer spades. Other men played chess or Scrabble. There was often a table filled with men doing some version of religious study. The Christians did Bible studies, while many of the Muslims seemed to favor teaching sessions with one man assuming the role of the teacher and the rest being students. Whatever the purpose of the gathering, the rule was six men maximum per table was strictly enforced.

Each table had six stools welded in place to its frame. Occasionally, someone would drag a plastic chair from inside his cell and make it the seventh seat at the table, but as quickly as a C/O noticed the addition, it would end with the inmate hearing, "Only six to a table!" shouted over the PA System or shouted in his direction by a C/O making rounds.

A DEGREE FOR HENRY

The barbershop was of interest as my hair needed a cut. Whenever I looked inside the converted cell that served as our barbershop, someone was in the chair. When it was finally free, I walked over and asked the man who was sweeping the floor how it all worked. I learned that D hall had two barbers, and he was one of them. Haircuts were free to all, with barbers being paid as cell house swampers (janitors). Upon more detailed questioning, I learned that the *free* haircuts came in only one style: the butch, I remembered from my youth. If you wanted a style cut, that required an informal tip to the barber. I was informed that tips ran from $1 to $4, depending how much style you required.

Since none of us had any cash money at Stillwater, tips were paid with items from the Canteen. The barber and I decided that a $3 tip would cover my required amount of style to be paid as two 12-ounce packages of cherry Kool-Aid and one package of white rice that I would obtain next week at the Canteen. Once the tip was available, my haircut could occur almost immediately.

Canteen was where we bought things, from toothpaste to playing cards, to sweatshirts; if we could buy it, Canteen was the place. Each prison ran its own Canteen and stocked several hundred items. We had no cash; the entire system was on paper. If we earned wages, we got a pay slip, and the money went in our account. If a benefactor on the outside sent us money, after the mandatory 10 percent deduction (for cost of confinement), the balance went into our account. Weekly, we went to the Canteen, and any purchases were deducted from our account.

I met several interesting people that weekend, from one guy seeking to borrow a full jar of Folgers coffee, the guy seeking to borrow a full pack of Pepsi, to the fellow needing some shampoo, and one fellow urgently looking for a partner for a game of chess. Everyone seemed friendly and almost ordinary.

I was just about ready to discard my mental image of prison life, the product of my life's exposure to Hollywood's many prison images filled with Jimmy Cagney's tough-guy images of the 1930, through my own youth's movies of prison wardens running illegal fight clubs. So far, none of it seemed to be holding true. Then, on Sunday afternoon, as I was walking on the back (east side) of the flag, I heard shouts from a card table. I turned to the sound just as one man reached across the table and punched his counterpart squarely in the mouth. The man receiving the blow yelled and lunged at his attacker. In less time than it takes to say it, both were rolling together on the floor.

In the background, I heard the C/O's radios blaring the alarm, and quickly, two D hall C/Os arrived, one from the east side C/O's chair and the other ran in from

CHARLES SLABAUGH

the west side of the cell hall. Both were shouting for the men to stop fighting. The fighters ignored them.

The two inmates continued to grapple, and the C/Os continued to demand that they stop for almost two more minutes until three C/Os, from what I later learned was "the squad," arrived. Red-faced and panting from their run, one of the new C/Os said "Stop it!" once. When the men ignored his order, the C/O pulled an aerosol can from his belt and quickly sprayed both men in the face. Immediately, they quit fighting and began to choke, gag, and rub frantically at their face and eyes.

About 20 feet away, where I stood with a group of onlookers, the four smell of the pepper spray he had used to such immediate effect was pungent and irritating. Without delay, the squad members handcuffed the two former fighters and stood them on their feet. One of the handcuffed inmates howled, "Get me some water so I can wash out of eyes!"

"Not here," said a C/O. "There's lots of water where you're going," he added. "But you guys need to understand that when we say 'stop,' it means to stop right now. Keep your eyes tightly closed, and it will burn less."

With that, the squad members, there were now five of them in the unit, marched the men out of D hall. Their first stop would be at the security center, where they would be evaluated for any medical attention. If they needed medical help, they would then go from the security center to health services. After that, they went to segregation: the hole. In their SEG cell, they would be interviewed by the discipline sergeant. The discipline sergeant would go over their situation and advise them of their options. It might go like this: "You were fighting, and we have it all on camera. If you want a hearing, you will get ninety, do sixty days. If, however, you'd like to be done with this here and now, I will offer you fifteen, do eight."

If the man agreed, he'd sign the paperwork and begin his eight days in SEG. If not, he'd wait for the hearing, which he would lose, and then do his ninety days. Almost everyone took the sergeant's deal.

If either man had been in a similar problem within a year, the penalties would be more extreme. For a second offense, they would be 50 percent more. For a third offence within a year, they would be double with the additional possibility of being transferred to the supermax at Oak Park Heights. Serious troublemakers usually found themselves at Oak Park.

A DEGREE FOR HENRY

When men emerged from their SEG sentence, they were ineligible to apply for any job for ninety days. This stopped their income and eliminated many of the benefits of being employed. During the weekdays, they were locked in their cell all day, which, to me, never was a good situation.

Listening to the talk after the fight, it had been about money. The card game had been for money, although none was visible on the table. The one guy had entered the game owing money from a loss the previous week and had just lost more. Apparently, the winner had asked when he would be paid, and the conversation had gone downhill from there.

The consensus of the spectators was that both men would get "fifteen, do eight." As it was explained, the segregation sentence would be for fifteen days, with the provision to serve eight days without further problem, and then to do the second seven days in a unit. If you stayed out of trouble for ninety days, the second seven days would be forgotten. If you got into more trouble, you would do the seven days you owed, plus the new sentence. By going to segregation (the hole), both men would lose their job assignments.

SEG I was told was okay. The cells were stripped bare, except for a bed, toilet, and sink. You could relax and unwind, and some of the men in the crowd thought that was okay. You were in your cell twenty-three hours a day with one hour out of the cell every day to exercise. Every third day, you could take a shower during that hour. To many inmates, it was an okay place to relax and recharge.

The worst part of going to SEG, the discussion went, was that after you finished your sentence, you couldn't have a new job for ninety days. This ninety-day delay in applying for a new assignment was a new wrinkle at Stillwater deigned to help those waiting for a job by reducing the pool of eligible men. In the past, men leaving SEG could immediately return to their job, if their job's supervisor agree. Recently, that had changed. Jobs were hard to find at Stillwater, and the system had about four hundred fewer jobs than was the inmate population. Going to SEG with this new system in place made it hard for many men to ever get back to an employed situation. When you did get hired for a new job, you started at the bottom of the pay scale. Going to SEG was costly.

I learned that the squad responded to all alarms: discipline and medical. The cell hall staffs were not supposed to get involved in breaking up fights. They would give verbal orders, "Stop fighting" or "Stop," but they were to wait for the squad's arrival, and then they were to allow the squad to physically stop the fight, if that was required. At Stillwater, from the time any alarm was sounded anywhere in the entire prison, all movements throughout the entire system stopped until the alarm

CHARLES SLABAUGH

was announced cleared. While the squad was dealing with a situation anywhere in the prison, no inmates were moving anywhere. Regardless the reason or excuse, no inmates went anywhere until the "secure" command went out over the radio network. At Stillwater, security was absolutely everything.

As I reflected on the fight I had just witnessed, it occurred to me that as soon as it was over, and the two participants were handcuffed and moved out to the security center and then to SEG, almost immediately, life returned to normal inside cell hall D. Card games resumed, the drill at the exercise machines started again, and phone calls were restarted or continued. What had been a break in the monotony of the day was over, and everyone quickly returned to doing whatever had been interrupted.

I had initially been surprised at how quickly the two D hall C/Os had responded to the fight. They seemed to come from nowhere very quickly. As I looked around, for the first time, I realized how many people were watching us all the time.

D house housed 196 inmates. During the time we were allowed out of our cells, from about 6:35 AM to 9:30 PM, with the exception of the noon and 4:00 PM count times, there were only five C/Os on duty in the cell hall. At any one time, one of these guards could be absent from the unit on a break or errand, but the other four remained in the unit. One would be at or near the front desk, which was at the main door, in and out of the unit. One was at a position at the front of the east side of the unit, essentially the unit's backside. Once an hour, two C/Os together walked the entire building, crossing every tier and looking into every cell. They always conducted these "rounds" with a partner, never alone. At all times each and every C/O had a radio on his belt, hearing every bit of traffic on the radio net. Their radios had a built-in sensor that noted if the radio became horizontal to the ground. If any radio went horizontal, that radio immediately broadcast an alarm to the entire network that directed everyone to that radio's location.

In addition, there were cameras everywhere – mounted on walls, they could see and record everything. Each camera took a picture every four seconds. If there was ever a question about what had happened, like what led up to the eruption of the fight we had all just witnessed, all the C/Os had to do was check the camera's record, and there it would be in black and white. Those time-and-date-stamped pictures would tell the whole story. The cameras could also be viewed in real time by any staff using any computer in the Stillwater network. In Stillwater, someone was always watching what you were doing, and there was always a record of what you had just done.

A DEGREE FOR HENRY

By the weekend's end, I had a fairly clear idea of how the system worked in my new neighborhood and exactly how much of a fishbowl I now lived in. I had met many inmates, most on just a first name basis: "Hi, I'm Bob" or "Call me Fortis." I had a clearer idea of my options.

Most of all, I knew that I wanted to get hired in a job, almost any job. So I poured over the green job application forms I had completed for the seven jobs posted as available. Before supper on Sunday, I tossed all seven applications in the mailbox.

Immediately after breakfast on Monday, I heard my name called to report to the front desk. As I descended the stairs, I hoped that I was being summoned for a job interview. The sergeant on duty said, "Pack up, you're moving down to the flag."

It was very warm up on the fifth tier, but I had met several men up there, and they seemed okay. I asked, "Why are you moving me?"

"Because the fifth tier is only for workers, and you're TU," came his immediate reply.

Without further conversation, I climbed back up to the fifth tier, packed my stuff into my gray plastic tub, and hauled it all down to the flag. In time I would learn that keeping all the unemployed in the same area made it easier for the staff to ensure that we were "locked in" for most of the day. All the unemployed men were grouped in a portion of the west side of the flag, right in front of the staff desk. Obviously, this was done for the convenience of the staff, not the inmates.

The fact that it was much cooler in the summer's heat living down on the flag made the quick relocation easier to accept, not that I had any choice anyway. One of the many perks of having a job was to live with the other workers, and being unemployed kept us down on the flag, very much in view of the front desk. Not that I planned to do anything very exciting anyway; the idea of living in a fish bowl never had appealed to me.

My first week at Stillwater passed slowly. All unemployed men were locked in their cells during the weekdays, except for meal times and a one-hour period in the early afternoon. For those of us who had just arrived, as opposed to those who had lost their jobs by going to SEG, we didn't get the hour out in the afternoon, but we got the evening hours after supper out, just like the men who had a job. That was helpful in allowing us to visit the gym or the yard, do some laundry, workout, or just hang out on the flag. That week I purchased a TV at the Canteen, which gave me another option to fill my days.

CHARLES SLABAUGH

Prison TVs were small with 13-inch screens, and the cabinets were clear plastic, with the entire insides exposed. I learned that this was done to prevent us from hiding things like drugs or homemade weapons in our sets. Inmates had a cable system offering about sixty channels, but none of the premium movie channels like HBO, Cinemax, or Showtime. I learned that the high telephone rates we paid (about 50¢ per minute, although a call to the Twin Cities was about 40¢ for fifteen minutes) paid the cable bill. I later learned that 60 percent of those high phone charges we paid were refunded to the DOC as a "commission." The DOC was very careful to ensure that no taxpayer funds went to pay for any luxuries like cable TV for inmates. Regardless, having channels like History, Discovery, and National Geographic was very nice. I now had a new option to fill my free time, of which I still had a great deal.

We bought TVs from the Canteen, and they were expensive. I had purchased a 27-inch TV from Walmart two years before for $188. Since then, electronics had gone down in price, but the 13-inch Clearview TV cost $249 at the Canteen. Many men had trouble coming up with that much money, but many also managed to get family or girlfriends to send in the necessary money to allow for the DOC's mandatory 10 percent charge on all monies coming in to inmates. That put the cost of the TV and the mandatory Minnesota sales tax at about $300 for those outside providers of the money.

After I had been in prison for a while, the logic of having TVs inside the prison came clearer to me. They were wonderful babysitters. The men who caused the most trouble inside the prison were those with little or nothing to do. At Stillwater then, inmates had three sports channels, which were very popular with most of the men, and a variety of rerun movie channels that also got a great deal of interest. We had enough variety on the network that almost everyone could find something of interest most of the time. Some men were just channel-switchers, spending hours flipping through all the channels, but even that exercise kept many of them out of trouble.

In some ways, having TV was almost an additional punishment for some of us. On TV, we got a good view of everyday life flashing on our screen every day. The exciting pace of modern life - new cars, lively social situations, and, of course, pretty girls that we no longer had any access to - were all paraded by our eyes every time we turned on our set. For many, it was a painful, constant reminder of the life they no longer participated in.

A disappointment came when the list of men hired for new jobs was posted at noon on Thursday, and I didn't get hired for a job. When the new list of available jobs was posted later that day, I got a new supply of the green forms and again applied for every open job. At least this time, I got two interviews.

The first job was for a tool room clerk in a welding shop. The interview went poorly. It was obvious to the staff member doing the interview that I knew nothing about welding. He quickly sent me back to D house. The second interview was in a wood industries shop, E shop. I was successful in getting hired, although I knew nothing about woodworking. The staff member interviewing me like the fact that I understood fractions and that I was older. He told me that older workers were more careful. On Thursday, my name and OID number was on the new hired list. I was delighted.

Friday morning, right after breakfast, I was paged to the front desk. "Pack up. You're moving to B East" was the message. Again, packing didn't take long. I was soon on my way to B East, which I found at the extreme northeast end of the Stillwater complex.

When it first opened, B house was a huge, long, double-sided cellblock housing over 530 men. In time, it was found that a cellblock with that many men presented too many problems to manage. The cellblock was split right down the middle becoming two long, single-sided units: B West and B East. The B East unit ran from north to south off the main Stillwater corridor, which ran east to west. The cellblock was on the east side of the building, and its east side was filled with industrial-type windows, most of which were cranked open in the July weather. From the cellblock's 256 cells, when you looked across the unit and through the windows, you had a view of the metal fence outside and the street beyond. It struck me as strange to be inside a densely-populated prison and see a normal street scene just outside the building.

When I wheeled my cart with my one gray tub and my new TV into the unit, B East's size literally took my breath away. The unit was four tiers high. Each tier had thirty-two cells. In the middle was a double stairway and then a second section of tiers, also four tiers high, for a total of eight tiers. In the extreme back of the building, almost a city block from the door where I stood, was a large gang-type shower.

In the middle, across the central stairway, was a large enclosed steel box with windows up high. I could see at least two C/Os inside. The C/O at the B East door told me to "Report to the bubble," pointing to that large steel structure.

CHARLES SLABAUGH

When I got there, I found a two-way speaker built into the wall next to a tray much like one would find at a drive-through auto bank. When I gave my name, the tray opened up, and a voice said, "Send in your ID."

I unclipped my plastic ID from my shirt and put it in the tray, which closed and retracted. After a few seconds, it extended and reopened, returning my ID tag and some forms with a room key. The voice said, "Cell 857," and immediately closed. The unseen C/O in the bubble had added a colored strip to the clip on my ID. That colored strip, I would learn, told all that I was assigned to D hall.

The information "Cell 857" didn't mean much to me. I could see that the cells on the flag to my left were numbered in the 100s, and the ones on my left were numbered in the 500s. As I stood there, an inmate walked by with a towel, a bottle of shampoo, and a soap dish in his hand, obviously heading for the showers in the back. "Can you point me toward cell no. 857?" I asked.

Without stopping or looking in my direction, he said, "Top of the rear section, near the back," as he ambled toward the showers.

I picked up my one gray tub, with my new TV on top, and climbed the right middle set of stairs to the top tier: tier no. 4. Near the end of the back section of the fourth tier, I found cell no. 857. The cell door stood open, and the floor was covered with paper and other trash. After checking to ensure that my new key worked in the lock on the door's padlock, I locked my tub and TV in the cell and returned to the flag. I pushed the flat cart back to the B East door and asked the C/O at the door to let me out so I could return the cart to D hall. "No," was his reply. "We'll see that it gets there. Just leave it here."

I next headed for the bubble. I had seen a swamper's closet in a converted cell by the center, double staircase, and when I got there, a swamper was sitting outside. I asked him for a broom and some cleaning supplies. His reply was, "No, you can get those at 3:30, when everyone comes back from work."

I explained that I was just moving in and that my cell was filthy. With that input, he said, "Okay, give me your ID."

Apparently, my honest face wasn't going to do me much good in this neighborhood, but at least I could clean up my cell.

Fortified with a broom, dustpan, a mop, a large bucket on wheels filled with soapy water, and some rags made from torn-up T-shirts and briefs, I climbed back to the fourth tier and began cleaning my cell.

A DEGREE FOR HENRY

B East was a working unit. Almost everyone who lived there worked in Stillwater's wood industries, run by Minncor Industries, or had a cell hall job in the unit, so B East was quiet that midmorning. As I cleaned, several inmates passed by without comment. Then a young black man stopped at my door. "Hi, I'm Smooth, and I live down there," he said, gesturing toward the front of the tier. "Are you new?" he asked.

I replied, "Yes, I just came here from D house. I have a new job in E shop."

He said, "You'll like B East much better than D house. These C/Os don't bother us much." Then he got down to business. "Do you have any coffee?" he asked.

As I had already learned how hard it was to avoid being taken advantage of in prison, I lied. "No, I'm out."

He replied, "Ain't it a bitch? My wife has been promising to send me some money for weeks, but she never does. When I get home, I'm going to kick her ass but good." With that, he walked off without waiting for my reply or comment.

It was already clear to me that coffee was a precious commodity at MCF – Stillwater.

I spent the first weekend getting to know my way around B East. In many ways, it was similar to D house, but when I tried to do my laundry Saturday morning, I learned that was going to be harder to do on weekends than in it was in D house. Almost everyone in B East had weekday jobs, so they waited to wash clothes until the weekend. The lines were long.

Two of the B East swampers were running a thriving business doing laundry for B East Minncor wood industries workers. The deal was simple: You provided a bag of soiled clothing, the necessary laundry detergent, and a Canteen item of $1 cost. While you were at work, they washed and dried your stuff, folded it, and put it in your cell before you returned for the day.

If anything, there were more card games in B East. I could tell that the stakes were high. With so many men working, there was more money in B East. This practice was completely contrary to stated DOC policy, but that rule was not enforced at Stillwater. Men passed Canteen items back and forth openly, and no one said a thing.

I was surprised and relieved that everyone I had met so far was so very polite. We were constantly in lines together; waiting for meals, the shower, a turn on the phone, or to just to get through the narrow door to enter or exit the living unit, and men were frequently bumping into one another's arms in passing on the narrow tier catwalks. Without fail, if someone brushed into you, he would immediately say, "Excuse me," and it was expected that you would do the same. It was true that every man in the prison was a convicted felon who had at some time intruded into someone else's space, but inside the prison, people were most polite and respectful of one another's space. In their day-to-day routine, it was a very polite world.

Chapter 3

E Shop

On Monday morning, I reported to my new job in E shop and met the boss, Bob. E shop occupied a huge room covering the middle third of the second floor of the Minncor wood industries building to the west of Stillwater's yard. This was Stillwater's original industry building and had initially housed Stillwater's first industry: a twine factory that had run for many years. The three-story masonry building had been well maintained and updated. It remained in active service despite being over ninety years old. I learned that the shop employed twenty inmates who were split up among seven workstations or, as they were known, workbenches. At each workbench, one inmate was the lead man. Acting as a foreman, he organized the workbench's activities.

There were four of us new men: all men Bob had interviewed and selected for his crew but really didn't know. To help sort us out, he gave us all a math test that was focused on fractions and carpenter's math.

Bob left us alone at a large picnic-type table, which I learned was used for breaks. The test was not a problem for me, and I finished quickly. One of the others, a man named Shepherd, was obviously having trouble. Seeing me sitting there, obviously finished, he asked me a question, then a second, and then several more. Bob was gone from the table. Wanting to be a good guy, I answered all of Shepherd's questions. It was apparent that fractions were a new subject to him.

Most of Shepherd's answers were wrong, so I helped him correct them. After we were done, he told me a bit about himself. He was from St. Cloud. He told that his being in prison *again* was, "completely bogus." He assured me that his lawyer

CHARLES SLABAUGH

was already at work on his appeal. He seemed very confident that he would soon be released.

In the middle of our conversation, Bob returned and quickly gathered up our papers. He left us for a few minutes but then returned with our working assignments in the shop. He complimented Shepherd on his math score and told him that he wanted him to try out the big table saw. That was an important job, Bob explained, as that saw cut up the dimensional stock for each workbench's jobs. Shepherd smiled at the news and winked at me. By Tuesday afternoon, I came to appreciate that my desire to be a good guy by helping Shepherd with his math test had really helped no one. Shepherd had turned several batches of raw material into worthless scrap, and Bob had quickly removed him from the big table saw, assigning him to another job on a workbench. No one was criticized and disciplined for this costly mess. It seemed to be accepted as just part of normal life in E shop.

Bob took me to workbench no. 4, and introduced me to Donte Armstrong. Bob explained that Donte was one of the shop's best men: experienced, dependable, and reliable. Bob told me to assist him and to learn all that I could. He emphasized that I should take my time. These tables that E shop made were custom products ordered by various Minnesota State county, township, school district, or city entities. They could specify the precise dimensions they wanted, the table top they needed (high pressure plastic, laminate, solid wood, or whatever) and the finish they preferred. Minncor would build them a custom table to their specifications. Donte made fancy large library and conference tables one at a time. Bob said that high-quality production, not high volume, was the important thing with this workbench. As we were introduced, Donte greeted me with a broad smile. He had a strong, confident handshake, and he seemed very friendly.

My working life had been spent in wholesale sales, most as a traveling salesman. I had never worked with my hands. I had never worked with a machine, other than a typewriter, computer, calculator, or an automobile. All around E shop, there were loud, noisy machines cutting, sawing, sanding, and planning wood. The noise level was high, and there was sawdust everywhere. I was more than a little bit intimidated with the noise and with the general atmosphere or organized chaos that I found myself in the midst of. This might take some getting used to.

When Bob left us, Donte smiled and asked, "What do you know about wood?"

"It floats" was my reply.

A DEGREE FOR HENRY

His smile grew broad. "Tell you what," he began, "just stay close to me, and I'll show you how to turn a pile of boards into a big, fancy table. There's really nothing to it if you're patient and careful."

I returned his smile, hoping that he was right.

As the weeks passed, Donte showed me the ropes and told me a lot about himself. He had worked with his hands all his life. He had made furniture, worked as a commercial painter and as a sign maker years before at a prison farm deep in Oregon's forests. He also allowed a lifelong addiction to heroin. Donte was a "lifer," serving a "life without the possibility of parole" sentence, but he still hoped to get out. "Someday, somehow."

Donte really did know how to work with wood. He not only understood the wood, but he also knew how to use the tools to the best advantage to get the most out of them. As the first week came to an end, I was more comfortable with him and with the job of working as his helper. Several of the other men in the shop were quick to point out that working as a helper/assistant would keep me out of the "big money," which was paid to the most experienced and productive workers, but that was okay with me. This kind of work was all new to me, and I was not very comfortable working with power tools.

One Thursday afternoon, we started a new project: a large conference table. Donte explained that this was a big job and a very important one. We spent the rest of the afternoon lining up the material we would need. Friday morning, we began shaping some of the parts we would need to fabricate to hold the massive table's top together. Donte told me to rough out some pieces from plywood using a hand saw. He showed me how to do it. After I had made a few pieces, he started finishing these rough pieces using a handheld, high-speed router. He was working right across the bench from me.

Donte seemed very relaxed, which surprised me because the day before, he had seemed very concerned and uptight, almost nervous about this very important job. For a while, all went well. I was cutting out the rough pieces we needed, and Donte was finishing them off with the router. After an hour or so, as I was cutting on a fresh sheet of plywood, a splash of blood landed on the sheet I was cutting. I looked up; to my horror, I could see that Donte's router's cutting edge had hit the side of his index finger on his left hand. The router's whirling tip was turning the area between Donte's thumb and index finger into hamburger, and blood was flying everywhere.

CHARLES SLABAUGH

Donte was staring at me. Then he looked down at the growing disaster. His face turned chalk white, and he let go of the router and the wood part, which was already splattered with blood. Then Donte dropped to his knees. Almost immediately, an alarm sounded, and men started shouting and running in our direction.

Donte collapsed on the floor, his eyes closed tight. His hand was bleeding at a rapid rate, and blood was pooling on the cement floor. Quickly, more C/Os came running; two of them carrying a large box with a red cross on the side. One of them took gauze from the box and began to apply direct pressure to Donte's mangled hand. Donte soon began to groan and mumble as he was trying to stand up.

The C/Os kept him on the floor until the blood flow began to slow under their direct pressure on the wound. Then two of them helped him to his feet. Then the three of them headed to the stairs that led out of the building. They loaded him on a John Deere Gator, and they headed for health services.

As they left E shop, I was almost numb. So much had happened so fast. I was just trying to understand what I had seen. A C/O began to yell, almost in my ear, it seemed, "Stay out of the blood! No one touch the blood! The blood-spill cleanup team will have to clean this mess up!"

In a few more minutes, the blood-spill team arrived to clean up. These were inmates who had received training on how to neutralize and clean up human blood spills. First, they blotted up the blood with saw dust, and then they sprayed the entire area with chemicals. Then they began shoveling it all into pink plastic bags, and they again sprayed the spots on the floor with more chemicals. Then they hauled it all away.

As this was going on, we could hear a siren's wail as the ambulance approached Stillwater's back gate to take Donte to the hospital. I thought in relief, *At least Donte is going to get some help.*

After almost an hour, a C/O ran up to me and shouted, "Where are Armstrong's sneakers?"

Up to then, I hadn't thought about shoes. In those days at Stillwater, all inmates wore white sneakers, but in the shop we worked in, steel-toe work boots. We walked to work in our sneakers and then changed to boots in the shop. At the end of each shift, we changed back to our sneakers for the trip back into the main prison.

A DEGREE FOR HENRY

The C/O's question about Donte's shoes told me he has gone no further than health services. I looked over to the workbench, and there sat Donte's and my sneakers on the floor. I quickly grabbed Donte's sneakers and gave them to the C/O. He ran out of the door with them in his hand. As he left, he said over his shoulder, "Security won't let him leave here in his steel-toes."

That really angered me. Even in the face of an ugly, major injury, security was still number one at Stillwater. I learned much later that, by then, the staff in health services had Donte's bleeding somewhat under control. The ambulance crew had given him a shot for pain, but his massive wound notwithstanding, until he got out of those steel toe safety shoes, Donte Armstrong was not going to leave Stillwater's close-custody umbrella for anywhere, not even a hospital's surgical suite.

The rest of the morning was mostly a blur to me. The blood spill team did their work, and Bob had me clean up the workbench area. Any lumber with blood on it went into the burn box, and that was about it. As we left for lunch, we were told that the entire E shop was "laid in" for the afternoon.

At lunch, the meal was strictly secondary to everyone telling their version of Donte's misfortune. There were many theories expounded upon. They ranged from Donte's ability to sue Minncor for millions of dollars to all routers being banned because they were so dangerous, to Donte was high on something, to Donte will probably be fired for his carelessness.

All we had was speculation; no one knew what had happened or why. In the context of a typically dull prison day, this day was quite the exception. We all had quite a bit to talk about.

It was several weeks before Donte returned. His hand was still in an enormous bandage. He had three surgeries and ultimately recovered most of the use and movement in his hand. I never did learn what had happened or if, in fact, he had been high that morning. He never did sue Minncor for anything.

The entire time I was at Stillwater, I heard many inmates enraged by some grievances, real or imagined, threaten to "sue the bastards," but very few suits were ever filed. The combination of most inmates having no money and the absence of clear recoverable records made such vows unenforceable. Often the inmate, in the heat of the moment, would say or do something that would land him in SEG. By the time he had endured that situation and the period following it when he was severely restricted financially and because he was locked inside his

CHARLES SLABAUGH

six-by-nine cell 24/7 because he lacked a job, he was effectively prevented from any effective follow-up or remedy.

My next week in E shop began with a meeting with Bob, the boss/supervisor/instructor. He said with a grin, "Well, you won't have Donte to show you how to do things for a while. I'm going to have someone else finish that big table. I want you to do three small commodes. Take your time. Ask questions. Whatever you do, don't get hurt! I'll be filling out paperwork on Donte's hand for weeks, and I don't want to do that again soon."

For the next few months, I worked in E shop. My work probably wasn't the best, but Bob said it was okay, and I didn't hurt myself. Almost all the furniture we built went to various Minnesota governmental entities. Some went to units in other prisons, but most of it went to city or county offices all over the state. We were told that they had no choice of vendors; by state statute, if Minncor made it, they had to buy it from us.

The work was dull, monotonous, and I was bored. After about six months, I saw a poster offering work as a tutor in education. I sent in an inquiry. Ultimately, I took a two-day tutor training course. I was hired as a tutor in a program called Lit 1.

Chapter 4

Literacy 1

There were four literacy classes, numbered 1 through 4. Lit 1 was the place for students with the lowest skills, and it also had many foreign students trying to learn English. These students were classified ESL, English as a second language.

In prison, not understanding English was a huge disadvantage. In the cellblocks, the C/Os were constantly giving verbal instructions over the PS system, such as "switch in," "chow," "the showers are off-limits," or "the door is open for the main yard." If an inmate didn't understand what was being said, he could find himself in the wrong place at the wrong time, and that could mean big trouble. In general, the C/Os were an unforgiving group. In most units, five C/Os worked each shift supervising inmates. They were busy, hurried, and often a bit on edge. If they told you to switch in and you didn't understand, you could easily and very quickly find yourself in handcuffs and on the way to SEG.

Many Lit 1 students were very unhappy to be forced to attend school. Under a new DOC policy, if an inmate didn't have a high school diploma, he was required to attend school until he earned a GED diploma. To earn that diploma, they had to pass five tests covering basic knowledge of math, science, reading, social studies, and English. In its current version, the English test was split into two parts. The first part was a multiple-choice exam on grammar and the rules of speech. The second portion required an essay on a subject mandated by the test. To pass the English portion of the exam, a candidate had to write an acceptable essay. If the essay wasn't acceptable, he did not pass the test. This was new, and the essay requirement had become a huge obstacle for many, especially for those in the ESL category.

CHARLES SLABAUGH

Most of these students realized that they were disadvantaged by lacking a diploma, but school had always been a problem in their lives, and they just wanted to get a job, earn some money, and be done with school. Also, being a student meant most of them worked only a half day earning at most $7.50 a week for fifteen hours. A cell house swamper, who had been on the job for a year, earned $1 an hour for thirty-five hours. Being in school embarrassed them and severely reduced their income. Plus, it was just very hard for many of them to pass the tests.

The ESL group was different. They realized the disadvantage they had by not knowing English well. As a group, they were eager to learn, hardworking, and grateful for the opportunity the prison's school program offered them.

The classroom had twenty oblong tables where tutors and students worked side by side. Later two additional tables were added. The plan was for each student to have his own exclusive tutor. This one-to-one ratio was effective, and it ensured that the students had the best chance to learn. In reality, the teacher, Jane Halverson, constantly hired more students than she had tutors, and several of the more capable or more motivated tutors frequently worked with two or more students simultaneously. Tutors came in various sizes, shapes, and with a wide variety of skill sets. Of the group in Lit 1, one tutor clearly stood out from the rest. Steven Kline was older than most in the room. He worked with two and sometimes three students, while most tutors were paired with just one student.

Steve Kline was friendly and had a quick smile, but he was all business in the classroom. As I came to know him, I admired the imaginative way he worked with his students. He constantly was coming up with inventive ways to keep his students focused on the task at hand, whatever that might be.

Once, when a Spanish-speaking student from Honduras was clearly not finding English books of interest to him, Steve learned that the student was interested in music from South America. Steve located a book in Spanish of South American songs, and then Steve set this student to work translating those songs into English. Once he started, the student began to share his translations with other Spanish-speaking students to their delight. In the end, his English skills improved enough for him to begin preparing for the English GED tests. In the regular world outside the prison system, candidates could take the national GED tests in many languages. In the prison system, English was the only option.

Steve's other student in the morning program was an extremely cantankerous older Mexican, Arturo Jacobs. Arturo was doing a long bit and had definite mental issues. He often seemed to live in a fantasy world of his own, and he would react dramatically when reality intruded on his world. It had been decided to keep

A DEGREE FOR HENRY

Arturo in school despite the fact that he was making absolutely no progress on his GED goals or with his proficiency in English. The daily routine of being in school seemed to keep him happy, content, and calm. Steven was semiliterate in Spanish, and he and Arturo communicated using bits of both languages.

Steve seemed to have the patience of Job as he kept Arturo working on lessons in very basic, simple English. Arturo never seemed to notice that he had been over the material several times previously, and he generally worked without complaint.

Arturo was quite a sight when he arrived for school every morning. His hair always a mess had not been cut for years. He shaved every morning, apparently thinking that part of his appearance was important, but never seemed to consider combing his extremely-long unkempt hair.

Arturo worked at about a second-grade level with his English. Steven's Honduran student, Emil, was doing high school work. Steven moved between them effortlessly and without complication. I admired Steven's work immediately, and over time we became good friends. Steve also worked two weekday evenings in Lit 1.

On Tuesday evening, Steve took a conversational Spanish class, which was also taught by Lit 1's Jane Halverson. I soon joined that class. Becoming more comfortable with Spanish would assist my tutoring work with our many Mexican students. Plus, anything that offered an alternative to my being in my cell was most welcome to me.

Jane was fluent in Spanish, having spent ten years as a Catholic missionary in Latin America, and she was very good at helping English speakers learn Spanish. I later learned that Jane was a Catholic nun who now worked for the DOC. As a young sister, she had gone to Latin America speaking English only and returned after ten years fluent in Spanish.

One Wednesday evening, Steve tutored a group of long-time inmates who held regular jobs under the old policy that had allowed men to keep jobs without having a diploma. Under that rule, they could keep their job only by attending night school one night of the week, with obtaining the GED diploma as a goal. I soon joined that group too.

I found myself living in a cell right next to Steve's in cell hall B West, the living unit where the tutors and higher-education students lived. I quickly got to know many of the men in the education group. A frequent visitor to Steve's cell was his friend, Henry Jiminez.

Chapter 5

Meeting the Group

Henry Jiminez was an interesting character. He was born in St. Paul of a Mexican mother and an absent father. At an early age, Henry had decided that he was gay. He quickly learned that being gay, especially in St. Paul's Latino community, was considered by many to be unacceptable. In school, as a boy, Henry was ostracized and sometimes attacked verbally and physically. Henry quickly learned to stand his ground and, if necessary, to defend himself. Winning most confrontations, he quickly developed a reputation as someone to avoid at all costs. If you started something with Henry, you faced a merciless and opponent.

Henry hurt many men, some of them severely.

Upon arriving in prison, Henry learned that general atmosphere was no less welcoming for homosexuals, but he also learned that the reality of living at Stillwater was such that his gay lifestyle presented him with the opportunity to satisfy his urges and to make some necessary money, if he carefully chose which men to deal with.

The mother of Henry was in a difficult situation, and she never had any money to send to him in prison. As a result, Henry never had much money, and as I had already learned, money was a very big deal inside Stillwater Prison. Henry met men with the perfect combination for his situation: They also had unsatisfied needs and had money.

In his second week at Stillwater, Henry agreed to meet an older man in his cell to perform fellatio for $10. They had hardly started when the cell door was jerked open, and four members of the squad interrupted their session. Just as quickly,

A DEGREE FOR HENRY

they both were off to SEG. In Henry's case, he got a sentence of fifteen days, do eight. That meant he could serve eight days of the fifteen-day sentence. If he stayed clear of more trouble for another ninety days, the seven days not served would be forgotten. If he got a new charge, the seven days would be added to the new charge's SEG sentence. The other man, who had many previous charges, got a ninety, do sixty sentence.

The discipline system within the Department of Corrections almost always included a provision to partially forgive part of the sentence if the offending inmate could avoid additional charges within the next ninety days. On many occasions, the first violation would result in a sentence of fifteen, do eight. A second violation would double the time to thirty, do fifteen. A third violation would go to sixty, do thirty, and so on. More serious charges, like using a weapon, would begin at 180, do 180 and increase from that. One student of mine stabbed his opponent with a pencil. The pencil was ruled a weapon by the discipline system, and the student did six months in segregation. Weapons charges always carried the danger of a transfer to the supermax at nearby Oak Park Heights. Weapons were not taken lightly at Stillwater.

The segregation unit at that time in Stillwater was located in the back half of cell hall A West. Roughly, this consisted of one hundred standard cells stripped of everything, except a bunk, toilet, sink, and a small mounted shelf for your hygiene stuff. The plastic chair and combination desk/wardrobe unit were gone, leaving only the essentials. You couldn't have your TV or radio in SEG, but after a long time there, you could borrow a radio that received just a few stations, if your behavior was good. You were in the SEG cell for twenty-three hours a day, getting one hour out for daily exercise. Every third day, you could take a shower during your hour out. There was little to read and nothing to do. SEG time was very slow time, and most men did their best to avoid it.

In Henry's first six months at Stillwater, he was in SEG three times; twice for being caught in homosexual encounters and once for fighting. He learned that while SEG time was pretty slow, there were ways to pass the time.

In SEG, men without money got a weekly issue of hygiene supplies. The "bag" contained toothpaste, a toothbrush, a bar of soap, a small bottle of shampoo, a deodorant stick, two no. 10 size envelopes and one large (8.5 x 11) envelope, a SEG pen (a special thin, flimsy pen designed for prisons and jails, much like a ballpoint ink refill cartridge without the pen's body; it was almost impossible to use as a weapon), and fifty sheets of plain 8 x 10.5 paper. Henry had some artistic talent. He was good at drawing some things, horses being a specialty. Henry learned that

41

he could fill many hours drawing horses in exquisite detail. That is what he did to fill up many days in Stillwater's SEG unit.

SEG was a noisy place. Those inmates living there would conduct conversations, shouting at the top of their lungs from cell to cell, often from tier to tier. The segregation staff was very busy delivering three meals a day, delivering mail, toilet paper, kite forms (a yellow form inmates used for any written communication with staff), and anything else the men would need, plus supervising each inmate for their hour out. If there was going to be trouble between inmates in segregation, it would occur during that one hour when they were out of their locked cell. As a result, the men were let out in small groups with the activity spanned most of the day and evening.

For control, the men were let out of their cells in groups of about four. They were restricted to a small area on each tier. Each tier had an exercise area and a shower. One at a time, inmates were secured (locked inside) the shower stall. This prevented many opportunities to fight and also prevented two men from getting into the shower at the same time.

Many men literally slept away the days in segregation. They would consume countless hours with a series of marathon naps filling up the daytime hours, with the exception of meal times and the mandatory hour out. Nighttime was party time. Once the sun set and darkness arrived, the noise level quickly came up.

Men shouted to their buddy, commenting on the meal just consumed: "Man, that was some shit! Someone ought to sue the commissioner . . ." And so it went until very early in the morning hours.

The day's mail might get discussed: "I got a letter from this cool broad. She told me about this great party last week. I got her name from Bubba in the kitchen. I asked her to send me a picture so I'd know what she looks like . . ." And so it would go until dawn was near.

With the approach of the sun, the noise would begin to taper off as more and more of the talkers dropped off to sleep. The arrival of breakfast might bring the volume up a bit, but as quickly as the meal was consumed, most of the men dropped off to sleep.

Nurses from health services were frequent visitors to segregation, delivering everyone's medications and insulin for the many diabetics. Deprived of almost all one-to-one contact in segregation, many of the men developed friendships with members of the medical staff. The segregation inmates eagerly anticipated the nurses' arrival, even if the visit was going to be very brief. The nurse would arrive, deliver the medication, and quickly move on to the next delivery. Most of the nurses, male and female, knew the segregation inmates by name and would greet them personally. To a man in SEG, where the SEG staff referred to him as "Cell 463," hearing "Hi, Mr. Larkin" was a big deal. Henry learned the ropes in the SEG unit and was quick to boast, "I can do SEG time with no sweat."

The truth was he truly hated his time in segregation, but he admitted that to no one.

As I came to know more people in B West, I met Dale Bishop. Dale lived one tier below me and was a constant participant in inmate athletics. Touch football, soccer, and softball, Dale played them all. A young, small man, Dale played all sports with an intense focus and skill. Dale first caught my attention at Sunday chapel, where he was usually up front, helping, lead singing, or offering prayer. Occasionally, he would act as an informal sergeant at arms.

Chapel was one of the few places where inmates from all units could come together at the same time. Under the controlled movement system, we went most places with our living unit only, but chapel was an exception to the policy. To get a chapel pass, men signed up a week in advance, and everyone with a pass could attend if they wished to. Using an informal but effective system of messaging, an inmate in A East would get a message to his buddy in D hall to sign up for Sunday chapel at 9:00 AM. They would arrive together and sit in the back. While the service was underway, they would visit in whispers in the rear of the room. The meeting might be quite harmless, or they could be exchanging contraband medications or even passing information about a gambling debt that some guy had skipped out on by going to SEG and then being moved into a different living unit. Now out of SEG, the man was now living in a new unit, far away from his debt, or so he hoped.

In a situation like that, the man trying to collect the money would pass the information on to a friend or fellow gang member in the debtor's new unit. Later, maybe a day or three later, the fellow who thought he had escaped paying would receive a visitor at his cell or possibly in the chow line at lunch. He would learn that his debt might be old news, but that was far from its being a forgotten or dead issue.

At that point, the man owing the debt had several options: He could make arrangements to satisfy the debt, or he could risk retribution from the friends of the man he was in debt to. One way or another, the debt would usually be satisfied in the end.

CHARLES SLABAUGH

One Sunday, as the service was underway, it became apparent to all in the chapel that three young men in the back row were not there for worship. They were having a fairly-loud conversation among themselves. Usually, such conversations were conducted in low, whispered voices, but these men were making no effort to be quiet or respectful in any way. As the service went on, their conversation grew louder and louder. They were clearly annoying the three outside volunteers who had brought in that morning's service. These outside volunteers were in a difficult spot. They had no real authority over us. They had the option of asking the C/O manning the chapel's entrance to quiet the men or to return them to their respective living units, but that would result in some form of discipline for those men and possibly could involve the volunteers in some form of controversy. If an inmate were sent out of the chapel, he could easily wind up in segregation, and the outside volunteers did not wish to be the cause of that for anyone. They were in a tough spot.

Suddenly, a small young man with close cropped hair left his seat in the front row and walked directly to the back, stopping right in front of the three men making all the noise. He knelt and began to speak in soft tones. "Fellas, please take your meeting out of here. We came to worship the Lord Jesus Christ, and you are making that difficult. We know that your conversation is important to you, but this service is important to us. I do not wish to be disrespectful, but I am asking you to stop what you are doing."

In amazement at his boldness, I held my breath, wondering what would happen next. At Stillwater, filled with murderers, rapists, and a multitude of antisocial fellows, anything was possible when someone intruded into what was obviously a gang's meeting. To my relief, one of the men making the disturbance, a man with gang tattoos and an authoritarian way about him, said, "Okay, we didn't mean to be rude. May we stay if we hold it down?"

"Of course," said the man I would come to know as Dale Bishop. "All are welcome to worship the Lord."

With that, he returned to his seat as the service continued. The gang meeting did continue but in much more restrained voices.

A few days later, I introduced myself to Bishop. We were in the main yard. I began by mentioning the scene in the chapel the previous Sunday morning and of my surprise and pleasure at its peaceful resolution. He smiled and said, "Well, they were just enjoying seeing their friends. They didn't want to cause trouble for anyone."

A DEGREE FOR HENRY

As we came to know each other in the years that followed, I learned that Dale was serving back-to-back "life without parole" sentences for a multiple homicide. He was doing drugs with two friends when the killings occurred, and now all three of them were at Stillwater.

In prison, facing an almost certainty of never being released, Dale had come to understand what a huge error he had made. He had decided to live as a Christian. With good support from his family, he was leading the best life that he could inside MCF – Stillwater. He ultimately earned his bachelor's degree and immediately started work on a master's degree.

Dale was a regular at Sunday Christian services. He worked on the Education Department's prison newspaper, *THE PRISON MIRROR,* and played in just about every sport offered for inmates. When asked about his very slim chances of ever being released, Dale would smile and wistfully say, "It's not up to me, but anything is possible with God's help."

In all the years I've known Dale, I have never known him to lie, cheat, or do anything that wasn't completely above board. For anyone to live every day inside Stillwater Prison as a Christian takes superhuman determination, discipline, and courage.

As I was learning about my neighbors, I was also learning about Stillwater. In 1853, the Stillwater Territorial Prison was created with a $20,000 appropriation of the US Congress. It housed all kinds of criminals and served the territory as its only prison.

In 1877, the famed Younger Brothers of the Jesse James Gang entered the prison after a botched bank robbery in the town of Northfield, Minnesota.

In 1912, construction of a new state prison was begun in Bayport, near Stillwater.

In 1914, Stillwater Prison opened in Bayport. A, B, and C blocks were built then, with D hall being built in the 1930s.

In 2000, when I arrived at Stillwater, the prison housed about 1,250 inmates, each man living in his own cell.

In 2003, Governor Pawlenty acknowledged his predecessor Governor Ventura's failure to keep the expansion of the prison system on track. The system was running out of room for new arrivals, and something had to be done quickly. Under Pawlenty's plan, five hundred cells were to be double-bunked at MCF – Stillwater, and also, five hundred cells were to be double-bunked at MCF – St. Cloud. Stillwater's cells were not perfectly uniform, but all were about 6 x 10 feet in measurement. Some were a bit larger, and some were a bit smaller, but all were completely inadequate for the two men who were then forced to spend almost all their time locked inside these small spaces.

To meet the demands of the state fire marshal, Pawlenty's announced goal of double-bunking five hundred cells was reduced to 160 cells at Stillwater and a reduced number at St. Cloud also. Initially, all the double-bunked cells at Stillwater were in B West.

According to the American Corrections Association, Stillwater's cells were inadequate for single occupancy. While no one ever seriously raised that issue regarding single habitation, from the outset, double-bunking was a trouble-filled prescription at Stillwater.

When double-bunking was being debated in the Minnesota Legislature, the only group to offer testimony in opposition to the proposal was the Correction Officers' Union. Those men and women who worked inside the prison every day knew, without a doubt, the chaos that would result from jamming mostly young men with testosterone in excess, men who had pretty much failed at life already, two to a tiny six-by-ten cell, and then locking them inside that cramped small spaced for long periods.

The politicians who had to decide the matter and were probably relieved at not being asked to finance the construction of yet another prison at a cost of several hundred million dollars. In any event, few seemed to think too hard on the issue. The chaos that followed was hard on everyone inside Stillwater's walls, inmates and state employees included. For a multitude of reasons, cell mates' individual living and sleeping habits irritated their companions in these forced marriages, and fights often resulted. In other cases, men were extorted by their cell mates, and instances of sexual assault occurred. Some battles were relatively minor; others were not with some men being injured in the extreme.

My work in Lit 1 took an interesting turn when the teacher, Jane Halverson, asked me to work with a young African, Omar Oogolala, a native of Southern Sudan. Tall, slender, with a head shaved completely bald, Omar had already caught my attention on the soccer field and at the chapel. He never missed Sunday services at the chapel and also attended several of the evening Bible study services most weeks. On the main yard's soccer field, Omar was an excellent player and a very serious competitor.

A DEGREE FOR HENRY

Omar was serving back-to-back life sentences for murder and was sentenced to "life without parole." While coping with a strange, new land; an inability to find regular work; trying to learn a complicated new language, English; and suffering from mental issues that have never been defined, let alone diagnosed or treated, Omar had murdered two people: his own young children.

From the start, it was obvious that he really needed help in mastering English, and Jane wanted him taught phonics. Omar quickly confirmed this, telling me, "I must learn the English."

Whatever I asked Omar to do, he did it or at least gave it his very best attempt. A refugee from Sudan's civil strife, he had come to America, hoping for a better life. Now he was in prison, probably for the rest of his life. It was ironical that he had escaped one ordeal only to arrive in another.

Omar knew his tribal language, he knew Arabic, and he knew enough Ethiopian to do business in a village market, but English was a huge problem for him. He knew enough basic words to survive inside Stillwater, but his fervent desire was to earn his GED. Optimistically, he spoke of then attending college.

The key to having a better living situation at Stillwater was to have a job. With a job assignment, a man earned a small income, but more importantly, he could spend much less time locked in his cell each day. On paper, having an assignment as a student was the same thing as having a job. Both qualified as an assignment, but in reality, they were not the same. Traditionally, student groups were made up of mostly younger men, and they tended to be harder to control. Because of that, the students' living units operated with different, less easygoing rules and regulations. Often students had a switch in to their cells earlier in the evening, cutting short the time for showers, making phone calls, doing laundry, or just relaxing over a card or board game. Also, students were paid a flat rate of 50¢ per hour. Depending on how long one had been on his job, men in other assignments could earn much more money and got periodic raises. Industry workers could earn as much at $2 per hour when they stayed with the assignment. Also, most student assignments were half days only, while almost all other assignments were for the entire day. For these reasons, for men at Stillwater, having a job was by far better than being a student, but the DOC's policy mandated that all men must have diploma to hold any job.

The policy came from the Minnesota Legislature, the folks who paid the bills. Under pressure from various businesses and other well-intentioned civic groups, the legislature had required the DOC to enact the diploma requirement. If an inmate could not provide proof of having earned his high school diploma, he had

CHARLES SLABAUGH

to earn a GED diploma before he could be considered for a job other than being a GED student.

The DOC had organized four classes: Lit 1, Lit 2, Lit 3, and Lit 4. Those men with the lowest level of skills, as defined by standardized testing score in reading and math, and those learning English went to Lit 1. Those with more advanced skills but still not at the GED level went to Lit 2. Lit 3 got the more skilled students and those actively working at the GED exams. Students with diplomas who were trying to prepare for college or trade school were placed in Lit 4, which was deemed the postsecondary group. The intent was that as a man-made progress, he would level up from one group to another until he had his GED.

Initially, when the GED requirement policy was being planned, the plan was for students to go to school all day, in the morning and in the afternoon, but there were too many men needing placement, so most became half-day students. It was thought that men would work on their studies in their cells during the half day they were not in the classroom, and in the beginning, the students were paid for the full day. Unfortunately, that seldom happened. Back in their cell hall and unsupervised, most men slept, played cards, or watched TV rather than working alone and unassisted on their studies. When that became apparent, the pay plan was revised, and the students only received pay for actual time in the classroom.

Omar Oogolala was the exception. Determined to succeed and earn his GED diploma, he worked every day in his cell. He still dreamed of going to college, and he wanted his GED now. Possibly exacerbated by the mental problems that had brought him to prison, his labors were not rewarded with much success. He found English very confusing. The same word could mean two or three different things, depending on the context in which it was used. The same-sounding word could sometimes be spelled different ways, again depending on how it was used. Omar and English were not a good combination, but he tried very hard every day.

English verbs were another big problem, and verb tenses were an even larger dilemma. He sometimes seemed to understand the difference between basic tenses – present, future, and past – but he frequently failed to use the correct tense when he spoke, using the present tense in all applications.

Nevertheless, Omar was always working hard in school to come up with the right word or phrase at the right time. Jane felt that an understanding of phonics was the key to helping him conquer the language. I did my best to help him find success with this confusing and complicated language: English.

A DEGREE FOR HENRY

As I was learning my job, I was also learning how to live in the cell block. The tutors lived then in a unit called B West, which contained 260 cells. In those days, each cell had one occupant. By chance, I ended up on the third tier of the back half of the cellblock, next door to Steven Kline, who was becoming a friend. Steve was an older guy also, and we both frequently walked the track in the main yard. Steve was clearly a leader among the tutors, or at least among the tutors who were trying to do a good job and help their students. I liked him, admiring the way he sincerely endeavored to help his students, and we seemed to enjoy each other's company. Living near us was Henry Jiminez, who had a job as a swamper, a unit janitor in B West. He and Steve were good friends, even though they had little in common that I could see.

Steven was friendly, quiet, and thoughtful; in contrast, Henry was brash, demanding, and openly gay, but they were close friends.

Henry was making 25¢ per hour on a thirty-five-hour week as a swamper. After the mandatory deduction of 5 percent to the victims-of-crime fund, this yielded Henry a weekly income of about $8.30. From this income, Henry had to purchase essentials, such as soap, shampoo, deodorant, laundry soap, razors, etc. Henry hated the dining room's food and preferred to cook himself, especially in the evening. To meet that expense, plus his almost overwhelming desire for new, brand name sneakers, sweat clothes, and other wants, Henry was always short of money, woefully short most weeks.

His family was of no help. His mother's situation was difficult, and she had long ago told Henry that she had no extra money. He had lost touch with his only sister, so Henry was on his own inside Stillwater. His homosexual behavior had long been a source of money, but such activities were dangerous in prison. If the C/Os caught you in the act, all participants went to SEG. One always had to be careful who they accepted as a partner. Disease was always a potential problem, and condoms were not available in prison. Stillwater had more than a few men who, at the conclusion of the encounter, rather than making whatever payment had been agreed to, would instead attack his partner.

Henry had experienced this problem and long ago had established a reputation as someone not to be taken lightly. It was well known that Henry would fight and that he was a relentless, fearless, dangerous adversary; one who gave much more than he received in a fight. In Stillwater's gay community, it was understood that Henry was not to be messed with.

CHARLES SLABAUGH

With nice New Balance or Nike sneakers going for $80 in the JCPenny catalog, having "dates" wasn't going to earn Henry enough money to meet his needs, so he was constantly looking for additional sources of revenue.

Being openly gay presented as a many problems inside Stillwater as it presented opportunities. Complicating things was Henry's determination to be accepted by all the leaders in the prison's population. Several prominent groups, among them Aryans, the Natives, and some of the Latino gangs, frequently exploited gays and often refused to do business with them. In some cases, they even refused to speak to them directly. Henry hated to be shunned like that, and he was determined to not only be accepted by them, but also to be treated as an equal by them. With that goal, Henry was always searching for ways to create situations where each group would seek to do business with him.

Food, drugs, and clothing were always in demand inside Stillwater, and Henry became a player with all of it. Several Natives working in the kitchen had access to food: meat, cheese, and good vegetables; and Henry got to know them. His initial contacts were rebuffed: "Stay away from me, Jen-Lo," one of the Native leaders told him. Refusing to take "no" for an answer, Henry kept talking, offering drugs he knew were available from some Latinos who were getting various drugs from the mental health professionals in health services. To get the pills, these inmates had to report to a function called pill run, where they reported to a window in health services and took the pill in front of a nurse. Upon demand, they had to open their mouth so the nurse could see that they had actually swallowed the pill. Their task was to pretend they had swallowed the pill and then to conceal it under their tongue or in their cheek during the inspection of their mouth. This was a bit uncertain and obviously unsanitary, but it was one way they could preserve these pills for resale. By trading food for pills, Henry established himself as a valuable connection and earned a new pair of Air Jordans to boot. Now he was rolling!

Getting people with a valuable commodity to trade it for another commodity that another group had was only part of the problem. Stillwater's system of controlled movement did an efficient job of insulating the prison's population from one another, dividing them into six groups that had almost no contact with one another. There were a few areas where men from all the living units could mingle with one another. The chapel was an obvious place where men from all units came together. Health services was another but only on a scheduled appointment basis, and inmates had no control of the appointment process. Education was another area of some overlap. So many inmates were involved with education as students, tutors, clerks, and swampers that they lived in three of Stillwater's six units. Henry did his best to use all possibilities to move merchandise, as he called it, throughout the prison.

A DEGREE FOR HENRY

The Stillwater security system, always watching everything through a network of cameras and a program of seemingly-random searches and pat-down inspections, was effective but not perfect. Sometimes, when a group was leaving an area, the squad would meet them at an exit door, requiring that all pockets be emptied, shoes removed, and then patting down the entire group. Also, anyone moving down Stillwater's main corridor had to pass through at least one metal detector under the watchful eye of a corrections officer. These components of the security system intercepted some of the unauthorized material and contraband that was always moving inside the prison but by no means all of it.

Henry's goal was to keep his merchandise moving and his personal income from the business interrupted without actually personally touching most of it. In this, he was never completely successful, but that was his ongoing goal.

Henry soon came to see that he was working in the wrong kind of prison job, at least if he wanted to make money. He had never given it much thought; he took whatever job he could get: swamper, painter, or just general laborer; he wasn't fussy. These jobs were easy, demanding little, but the pay was too small, from 25¢ to a top of $1 per hour. As he looked into it, some jobs in education paid more, up to $1.50 for tutors and clerks. In Minncor shops, men earned as much as $2 per hour in some jobs and even more in a few jobs in a new category of jobs classified as interstate. Soon Henry was applying for those kinds of jobs.

The weekly Stillwater inmate job posting was on the bulletin board by noon of Friday. It was posted in each living unit and listed all open jobs. Interested inmates scanned the list, and many applied for open jobs in shops or living units where they had friends living. The idea was usually to get with their buddy so they could spend free time together. In addition to listing the jobs and telling which unit they lived in, the posting told what, if any, special skills were required for each job. Some jobs, welders for example, required obvious skill sets. Others, like some of the Minncor clerk assignments, might require special computer skills, and those requirements were also shown on the posting. Still other jobs, like those in education, required high scores in reading or math, and those requirements were also listed on the posting.

These scores came from testing that all men took at the intake process at MCF – St. Cloud. Those scores were updated when men took and completed any education courses, so the information was generally up-to-date.

Henry completely ignored any and all information about the skills required for any of the posted jobs. If the pay range suited him, he applied for the job, regardless of any skills listed as necessary or preferred. For several weeks, Henry filled out an

CHARLES SLABAUGH

avalanche of the green job request forms and wasn't hired for any of the sought-after jobs. "Just another example of discrimination," he thought. "They don't want me because I'm gay, Mexican, or both . . ."

The more he thought about it, the more determined he became to get a better job. In Henry's mind, he was entitled to a better job. He was convinced that it was his right.

One evening Henry was visiting with his friend Steven Kline. Henry brought up the issue of seeking a better-paying job. Steven confirmed that he earned $1.50 an hour as a tutor in Lit 1. Henry's response was, "How can I become a tutor?"

Steven pointed out that the tutors had to have reading and math scores at grade level 13, college level.

"That's bull," Henry replied. "That's just a way to keep guys like me out. Anyway, what I really want is a Minncor clerk's job. They go up to $2."

Steven quickly replied, "You won't get one of those jobs either. They require computer skills."

Again, Henry's answer was, "That's just more bull. They just want to keep those jobs for white guys."

Knowing Henry well, Steven smiled and told his friend, "Henry, if you really want one of those jobs, you need to come back to school and get your skill set improved." Steven went on, "You really ought to get in the Spector program in education and earn a college degree."

That comment stopped Henry dead in his tracks. "A college degree," he stammered. "You really think that I could do that?"

Steven said, "I know you could do it, but it won't come quickly or easily. The best part of Spector is that, in here, they treat it as a job. You get paid in the morning for going to classes, and in the afternoon, you go to the Spector room and study or work on papers and reports, and you get paid for that too."

Henry quickly countered, "Yeah, but you only get the student rate: 50¢. I can't make it on that."

"I know that's tough, but what the hell, you're at 25¢ most of the time anyway because you're always starting over at the bottom of the scale with a new job,

A DEGREE FOR HENRY

because you just came out of SEG. Henry, the best part of earning a college degree would not be what it does for you in here but what it would do for you when you get out of prison in five or six years."

"Seven," Henry interrupted.

"Well, whatever," Steven answered. "You're getting out someday, and just imagine how hard it will be to get a job on the streets after all the years in here, especially with zero job skills. What job do you want at the Como Avenue Car Wash? Just imagine if you had a college degree, an AA degree with some real job skills. Get into Spector and you can make something happen, my friend."

For the next few weeks, Henry and Steven continued their debate during their time back in B West. Henry was fearful; he sincerely believed that because he was a Mexican who was also gay, life's system would never allow him to succeed at anything worthwhile. Steven knew that there would be challenges, roadblocks, and that there was always prejudice in life, but Steven also knew that the world was changing, that, in fact, it had already changed substantially since he and Henry had first come to prison. He also knew that Henry was a fairly bright guy and had never had much of a chance in life and who really had little education. The fact that he had earned his GED diploma in prison proved that he could do it. In prison, many men attend GED classes – they had no choice – but few found success. Henry's diploma and his many hours of conversation with him convinced Steven that Henry could do it and find success from college work.

Finally, after several weeks of back-and-forth, Henry, with Steven's help, completed the application for Spector and dropped the application in the mailbox. That evening Henry treated his friend Steven to a supper of burritos. Henry made them from his mother's recipe as best he could. Where his mother used fresh pork and rich, fresh tomatoes, Henry had to use a stick of summer sausage from the Canteen. He did have tomatoes, skimmed from a shipment from his contact with the Natives and headed for an Aryan customer in B East. He and Stephen relished the special meal and the feeling of accomplishment that engulfed them as they savored the success they anticipated to be coming Henry's way soon.

Two days later, Henry returned to his cell after the afternoon's work and found a printed notice on the floor of his cell, informing him that he had not been accepted in the Spector program.

Under the column marked "Reason for Rejection," two boxes were checked. One cited "Inadequate Reading Score" and the other specified "Inadequate Math Score." A line at the bottom of the form urged, "You are encouraged to work on

CHARLES SLABAUGH

your skills and to request retesting when you are ready to update your test results." It went on, "Please be advised that you may only take tests every ninety (90) days."

To Henry, this was confirmation of what he had feared all along: He had no chance. The system was aligned against him completely. Here, in prison, or later when he got out, he would always be Mexican, gay, and most of all, poor. The unfairness of it all infuriated him and almost made him physically sick.

He stormed over to Steven's room and thrust the offending notice under his friend's nose as Steven reclined on his bunk. Steven immediately read it and sat up. "This doesn't mean a thing," he began. "You need to write a kite tonight to Ms. Polinski, the education director, and tell her—"

"She won't help. They don't want me," Henry interrupted. "I'm just another dumb Mexican to her."

"Not so," Steven shouted back. "You don't understand. Spector always needs students. They are constantly ignoring their own rules to keep the classes full. To collect the money they need to run the program, they have to keep the chairs full in all the classes. Their funding comes from the federal government, and it is based on classroom hours of instruction, how many students are in each class times the number of hours that the class meets. What you do tonight is write a clear, well-thought-out kite to Ms. Polinski, and maybe one to Norma Kolkins too, she's the Spector administrator, and tell your story. Believe me, Henry, in this case, no doesn't mean no."

What Steven didn't tell Henry was that he had an excellent relationship with Pamela Polinski. He called her Pam, and she called him Steve, and he planned to talk with her the next morning. By luck, on his way to work the next morning, Steve saw Ms. Polinski in the main corridor. Steve quickly made his case.

Ms. Polinski listened to Steve's appeal: "Henry was smart. He was determined to better himself. He really wanted to enter and complete the program."

Pam Polinski didn't know Henry Jiminez, but from the name, she knew he'd be classed as Hispanic. To Henry, that would have sounded bad, an invitation to discrimination, but to Pam Polinski, she knew better. Everything in the DOC was PC, politically correct. The population of the DOC's inmate group was about 50 percent people of color. Under the rules, every cellblock, every job assignment, and every class in every department, including education, had to reflect those numbers. Finding enough "men of color who were qualified to take college classes was never easy. Those numbers, the percentage of men in the program, had to be met. If academic requirements had to be modified to meet the numbers, so be it. This was not a new problem, and Pam Polinski made a quick decision.

"Oh," she began, "but how is Jiminez on discipline?"

Steven frowned. "He has been in and out of SEG a few times, but nothing lately. He's no angel, but he's smart, and he really wants to do this."

Ms. Polinski said, "Okay, I'll see what I can do, Steve."

And with that, she was off to her first meeting of the day, which was to begin in three minutes.

The next afternoon Henry found a new printed notice on the floor of his cell. He had been accepted into the Spector program, despite his low scores in reading and math. He was advised that the new assignment was effective in two weeks and the semester's classes would begin a week later.

That night he and Steve celebrated again. No burritos this time – feasts like that took time to organize – but this time they celebrated with Pepsis and popcorn. They savored Henry's enrollment in college and what they both hoped was the start of a new and better life for Henry.

As they enjoyed several bags of microwave popcorn, Henry complained to Steven about a problem that had occurred in his merchandise business. Henry needed to get some pills that a mental health patient in D hall was trading to a Native in A East. The problem was who could move the pills from one unit to the other. With the controlled-movement system, it was hard, often impossible, for an inmate to go from one living unit to another at will.

Henry realized that Dale Bishop, who worked on the inmate newspaper *The Mirror*, could do that easily if he was on business for the newspaper. The previous Sunday, Henry had gone to the religious services center, the chapel, to talk with another inmate. He had run into Dale and made his request. Speaking in a low, hushed voice, Dale explained that he could not do that because he believed that no one should be using (misusing) drugs. Henry had tried to talk Dale into doing what he wanted, but to no avail. As Henry put it, "That dumb fuck is really trying to live as a Christian. He'll have lots of luck with that in here."

Steven was a serious Roman Catholic, and he bit his tongue, not wishing to offend his friend, a fallen-away Catholic. Steven knew that Henry would not be swayed on this subject. He had often told Steven, "The only God I believe in is me," and Steven knew better than to fight that battle right then.

At that moment, Steven was in extreme physical discomfort. He had eaten a lot of popcorn, all bathed in salt and butter; plus, he was on his second Pepsi. Steve was having a problem keeping that, plus his supper of a chili-covered hot dog safely in his stomach.

He had been having stomach trouble for some time, and tonight it was extreme. The prison doctor, an older gentlemen named Blumenthal, had diagnosed the trouble as acid reflux, and he had prescribed a popular drug: Zantac. Steven had seen the doctor earlier that week and had asked for a Zantac refill, but it had not yet been delivered from the DOC's Oklahoma pharmacy.

Steven always found it interesting that their pharmacy was four states away, but years before, the Minnesota Department of Corrections had contracted all their medical staffing to a third-party provider. All doctors, nurses, dentists, psychiatrists, and physical therapists worked for that firm; their pharmacy was in Oklahoma. Regardless of who was doing it, that night Steven wished the drugstore was closer. He had a very great pain in his belly that night.

For two weeks, Henry Jiminez dreamed and fantasized about what life after prison, with a college degree, would be like. He'd have a good car, not just a nice car. He dreamed for something sexy and hot. Also, he dreamed of a fancy apartment and a really special girl friend. Yes, Henry liked girls too; his preference was really for men, but as the saying goes, he could go both ways. Either way, his life was going to be better – a great deal better. Of that, he was growing more and more certain.

Two weeks later, Henry dogged Steven at lunch. It had been the first day in the program, and he was angry. He was doing this to learn computer stuff so he could get a higher-paying clerk's job in a Minncor shop, but the first day in the Spector meeting, Norma Kolkins, the Spector program director, had told them that all of them would be taking various courses as part of the requirement to earn an AA college degree.

"This is bull," Henry stammered. "That bitch said we need to take English, history, math, and anthropology this year. I don't want to waste my time on that crap . . . I want to learn computers."

Steven gulped and waded into the issue with determination. He had explained to Henry that degrees offered in the program, while offering a major in, say, business,

A DEGREE FOR HENRY

these were general education degrees. To meet the program's requirements, it was essential for everyone to take work in several subjects. These were essentially general education degrees.

Steven pointed out that they had discussed all this before and Henry had agreed to all this. Steven went on, that it was true that computer skills would lead to a better job in prison, but he again argued that the real objective here was the college degree for when Henry was released.

With great effort, Steven convinced Henry to return to the Spector room after lunch for the afternoon's session. Henry's first reaction was to say, "Fuck this. This isn't what I agreed to, I quit."

Steven talked him out of that by emphasizing the reality: Henry was going to get out of prison someday. They continued to talk after work/school and through a meal of ramen noodles in hot chili flavor and many cups of coffee.

Henry was adamant that he didn't want to do this, all Henry wanted was computers, and Steven was equally adamant: "You must do this to find success and build the kind of life that you want to have outside of prison. Above all, you never want to come back to this awful place."

In the end, Steven won the battle. Henry agreed to continue the program, and Steven agreed to help him through any portion of it that was too tough. By the end of the supper and of the evening, Steven's stomach was on fire. The chili noodles and the coffee's acid had badly irritated his acid reflux problem again, and again, he was out of Zantac. Steven later became nauseous and lost supper after he was alone in his cell. He slept fitfully that night.

Most observers of the unusual relationship between Steven and Henry would, at some point, wonder as to Steven's motivation to make such an extreme effort to help Henry, who was difficult, demanding, and often arbitrary. Steven had been a tutor in Lit 1 for many years. He had seen many come into the program and fail, accomplishing little or nothing. He has long ago decided that Henry was bright enough to succeed, and most importantly to Steven, he saw that Henry was determined to succeed. Henry was unwilling to accept his low station in life. Steven had long ago vowed to himself that he would do whatever was necessary to help bright, determined men escape the pit of failure and loss in which they found themselves inside Stillwater prison.

In a few days, Henry brought his first semester's schedule to show Steven:

CHARLES SLABAUGH

English Writing & Research	4 credit hours
US History, 1776 – 1866	4 credit hours
Cultural Anthropology	4 credit hours

Henry was unhappy again. There were no computer courses; plus, he didn't even know what anthropology was. Steven patiently explained that the computer courses would come later, probably next semester. Steven knew that all of the Spector room's computers were going to be updated with new hardware and software, but he didn't want to tell Henry that for fear of confusing him further with the idea that the equipment wasn't the best available. He did explain that the study of anthropology was the study of how cultures lived. Henry was still not thrilled, but he finally said, "Okay."

As Henry's college career was beginning, I was getting to know Omar Oogolala, my newest student a little better. Like many students in Lit 1, Omar Oogolala had missed many of the fundamental building blocks of the education process. He wanted to do math at a high level, but he didn't know his basic mathematical multiplication tables. He wanted to write his story – the narrative of his journey from South Sudan to Minnesota - but English verb tenses were mostly a mystery to him. Most of all, he wanted to pass the five tests in the GED process, but to even qualify to begin taking those tests, he must, per the new DOC policy, raise his reading and math scores a lot.

Omar was trying hard, very hard. Despite his desire to learn, his brain didn't seem to be cooperating. He would do the daily drills, exercises, and workbooks prescribed by Jane and me, but nothing seemed to stick. We would spend an afternoon on math tables. By 3:15 quitting time, Omar would seem to be getting them fairly well. When the next morning arrived and I would begin to quiz him on those same tables, Omar would pretty much draw a blank. It was frustrating to me. Worse, it was demoralizing for Omar. Many times he wished out loud to be able to just quit school and take a job, but the DOC's policy was firm. To get any job, you must have a high school or GED diploma. With that reality, plus our own desire to succeed, Omar continued to work with, at best, only marginal success.

To even qualify to begin taking those tests, Omar had to raise his reading and math scores by a considerable amount. A new DOC regulation mandated minimum scores on both tests before anyone could test. The reason for the new policy was simple: money. The practice and real GED tests cost money to take, and then to be officially scored by the GED office, DOC was paying a lot for failed tests. By

A DEGREE FOR HENRY

raising the requirement to test, they would improve their percentage of successful testers and reduce overall cost.

Other tutors in Jane's Lit 1 class had equally-difficult situations with students who seemed unable to learn or retain information. In private sessions with the tutor group, Jane told us that the DOC estimated that 80 percent of Lit students were classified as learning disabled. The disabilities came in a confusing collage of types and forms and from many different causes.

Some came from congenital conditions, some from drug or alcohol use/abuse, and some were the result of injury; but the reality was that many of these men could not do work at this level or could do it only with great difficulty.

With Omar, I did my best to find ways to improve his results and overcome his problems, but to no or at least small avail. Despite many different attempts by Jane and me, and Omar's tireless enthusiastic efforts and unwavering cooperation, many things seemed beyond his grasp.

One summer, as the semiannual graduation ceremony approached, Jane told me that Omar was going to get an award at the ceremony. At these twice-a-year exercises, in addition to those earning certificates and diplomas, a few tutors and clerks were awarded a certificate for doing a very good job. One or two students were also honored with induction to the National Adult Honor Society for generally unspecified accomplishments. Those students were generally men like Omar who tried very hard but accomplished little. They made a sincere effort but accomplished little, and the Education Department wanted to encourage them.

Graduation day finally arrived. School was cancelled for the afternoon period so that the teachers and those being honored could attend. For the ceremony, Stillwater's visiting room was used as the venue. The furniture was rearranged, with one area for inmates, another area for invited guests: friends and family of those being honored. All chairs were pointed toward a portable rostrum that had been brought in for the occasion. At the appropriate time, each unit announced its movement for graduation, and those inmates with passes began moving to visiting room. Leaving their cells, showing their passes at the unit's door, they proceeded on to shakedown and then into the visiting room itself. At the visiting room, they showed their pass and were admitted to the room. A C/O directed each inmate to the seating area reserved for him. Once they were all seated, the visitors came in and were directed to their seating area. Wives, mothers, fathers, grandparents, and girlfriends came in, all eagerly scanning the inmate groups looking for their honoree. Graduates and others being honored were allowed to invite two family members or one friend. To be admitted, all outside guests had

CHARLES SLABAUGH

to be on an inmate's list of approved visitors. Smiles were exchanged, but at this point, contact was not permitted.

I was receiving a tutor award. When I entered the room, I immediately saw Omar Oogolala sitting alone on the end of a row. I took the empty seat next to him and said, "Hi."

His response was, "Why am I getting this award?"

I smiled and said, "Because you work very hard. You are an exceptional student."

He had no reply.

The program was short. The warden welcomed all and introduced an assistant commissioner from St. Paul. He then introduced the education director, Ms. Polinski, who welcomed all and introduced the first speaker. A former student who had earned his GED long ago and had stayed on in the department as a tutor, his talk was short, emphasizing that school was a wonderful place to prepare for success. Ms. Polinski then introduced the main speaker, a community leader from Minneapolis. His message was one of encouragement, urging all to use their new skills once they returned home to help make their communities a better place to live and work.

Ms. Polinski then introduced her VO – Tec teachers, each of whom then explained their program – carpentry, welding, and computers – and then called up each man from each group to be recognized. The teacher handed each man his certificate, shook each man's hand, and then the group applauded. Ms. Polinski then introduced the head of Literacy, my boss, Jane Halverson. Jane explained how important the tutors and clerks were to the program and then called up those who were being honored from the group. Next came the GED group with thirty-two men receiving a diploma that day. Jane then explained that a group of students were being honored by induction into the National Adult Honor Society. When his name was called, Omar joined the group, a somewhat confused look on his face.

Jane gave each Honor Society honoree a certificate. She went into great detail explaining why each one was being honored, reading the nomination submitted by each of their teachers. She made each man sound very special and unique.

She then explained that they each would receive a lapel pin from the Honor Society. Because the pins were metal and contained a sharp, potentially-dangerous edge, inmates ("offenders") could not have the pins in their possession while in prison.

A DEGREE FOR HENRY

The men could either give the pins to their guest(s) to hold for them, or they could have them mailed out to someone else. I immediately thought of Omar. He had one relative in the United States, a brother in St. Paul. The brother visited maybe once a year, and Omar had trouble getting him to accept his prepaid telephone calls. The rest of Omar's family (father, mother, and four sisters) were in a UN refugee camp in Ethiopia. I felt sad knowing that Omar would never get his pin.

Jane congratulated the three Honor Society members. The crowd applauded, and the three inmates returned to their seats. When he sat down, Omar turned to me and asked, "Now can I take the GED exams?"

I said, "No, this is just Jane's way of telling everyone what a good student you are. She appreciates how hard you work in class."

Looking very grim, Omar said, "I would rather get the GED."

With that, Ms. Polinski congratulated all and invited everyone to the refreshment area. The men with visitors moved to join them, and those without headed for the table spread with cookies and sliced cake. Several Lit teachers were manning the table, making an effort to see that the inmates got only one free cookie and slice of cake and only one cup of Kool-Aid punch. Theirs was a difficult job as many of the inmates literally jammed the treats into their mouths and immediately rejoined the line. Free cookies and cake were not ordinary fare at Stillwater, and for most, this was an opportunity not to be wasted.

The editor of the Stillwater *THE PRISON MIRROR* was in attendance with the Education Department's digital camera. The Education Department also brought the one graduation-styled cap and gown that it owned to the ceremony. One by one, many of the honorees donned the cap and gown, often with a beaming parent, grandparent, or girlfriend on their arm, and the editor snapped one picture. Later those pictures would be given to the men. For many, the picture in the cap and gown was the day's absolute highlight.

As quickly as it had started, it was over. In groups of four, the inmates left the visiting room for the shakedown room next door. In shakedown, under direct supervision of a C/O, each man underwent a complete strip search, complete with a cavity search. This was standard fare after any contact visit, where an inmate met with anyone from outside the prison, and it went fairly quickly.

The entire exercise was an efficient, well-orchestrated program. In two hours, seventy-six men had been individually honored, refreshments had been served, and security needs had been met. Omar went through shakedown with me. As we left the shakedown room to return to our living units, he still had a confused look on his face. I wondered what he would do with his Honor Society certificate.

A bright spot soon entered Omar's life when a new tutor, Donald Jergens, joined the Lit 1 group. Tall, with a mop of unkempt hair that he never combed, let alone cut, Don Jergens was a lot of fun. Doing a long sentence, (or bit, as it was referred to, Don had earned his GED quickly and was hired as a tutor. As he explained to me, despite having a mother who made a career as a teacher and having a sister who also taught, he had never taken his own education seriously. He said, "First, I discovered girls and then meth. After that, I was done with school."

When his life finally imploded, and he found himself in prison literacy classes, he easily passed the GED exams. With his new GED diploma, he quickly found work as a tutor.

Don quickly established himself as a popular leader in the class. With a creative mind, Don was trying to become a writer, with poetry as his special interest. With Jane's agreement and encouragement, Don created an evening poetry group that met on Tuesday evenings.

Somehow Omar decided that he was interested in joining the group. While nothing that the group produced probably compared favorably with the works of Keats, Shelly, or Lord Byron, the group proved to be a wonderful outlet for several of the men, Omar Oogolala in particular. For Omar, the effort seemed to open a door for him, a door that he enjoyed immensely.

Omar quickly purchased a new three-ring binder from the Canteen and began to collect his poetry. Don Jergens worked with him, encouraging his works and congratulating his creativeness by overlooking his many errors in spelling and grammar and focusing on his message. Don became very important in Omar's frequent battles with depression and discouragement. From my perspective, I saw even more enthusiasm in Omar's classroom work and an obvious brightening in his overall mood.

Steve Kline had an unhappy friend on his hands when Henry Jiminez started his classes. In Henry's opinion, English Writing & Research was a "pain in the ass, all we are doing is writing dumb stuff. History is stupid. Who cares what year the war of 1812 ended? And anthropology is just a bunch of crap about people who never amounted to anything." Henry was not a happy camper. With a sigh, Steven started to go through it all again: The goal was a college degree. It would make a huge difference in Henry's life when he got out of prison. It was the only thing

A DEGREE FOR HENRY

Henry could do to separate himself from the pack. It was the best thing Henry could do to ensure a good job and the kind of life he dreamed about.

Henry again agreed to stay in the Spector program, and Steven again promised to help. Steven started to spend a great deal of time in the evenings and weekends with Henry, helping him do the many papers that a college education is all about. Henry's English skills weren't bad, but he had never done any writing of this kind. Footnoting quotations, preparing bibliographies, and the other tools of a college term paper were all new to him; so Steven helped his friend.

Steven was still having major troubles with his stomach, and the doctor was growing more concerned. Steven had sent him a new request for Zantac, and Dr. Blumenthal said that he was going to send Steven to the hospital for a test. The doctor wanted to send a small camera down his throat to the connection with the stomach and then to slowly bring it back up, examining everything. When Steven asked why, the doctor's reply was noncommittal, "You're using a lot of Zantac. I just want to look everything over and see what's going on." That didn't sound like the whole story to Steve, but he left it there.

As Omar dug into his new interest, poetry, during his free time and continued to labor during the day at his English skills in class, Henry continued his many other activities. During the morning, he was in class or study hall, and in the afternoon, he worked in the Spector room, trying to do all his reading and to make notes to discuss in the evening with Steven. Henry made note of words or phrases that he didn't understand, and he would rush to Steven's room after class and immediately begin to bombard him with questions.

Henry had experimented using the dictionary, trying to explain words he didn't know. Too often he found that the dictionary's definition didn't really help. Many times the definition in the dictionary used additional words that he didn't know, and that just increased his confusion. When he could talk with Steven, it seemed that he understood the words quickly and completely, and he was also enjoying the extra time with his friend Steven.

His biggest problem was in preparing the many papers his new instructors were requiring. Henry's idea was to read the material, read the question, and then write the paper. Steven explained that to finish with an acceptable paper, time must be spent on preparation and organization. He showed Henry how beginning with a good outline led to a more cohesive and concise paper. The length of the papers presented problems. If the instructor asked for twelve to fifteen pages, Henry focused on "twelve" as his goal. Steven took the position that answering the question or questions was much more important. He showed how the number

CHARLES SLABAUGH

of pages or words used was less important than the issue of how thoroughly and completely you answered the question.

Their conversation during these sessions was colorful and very animated, with Henry always resisting Steven's suggestions in the beginning. In the end, however, Steven would win Henry over to his position. Henry admitted to himself that his papers were improving as the semester moved to its conclusion.

Henry's grades in his courses were improving too. On his first paper in English Writing & Research, he got a C-, with lots of angry-looking red ink from the instructor. His midterm paper came back with a grade of B and fewer red words from the instructor, which pleased both of them.

The weekly quizzes he took in some classes were another problem. Henry was not used to remembering small details from things he had read, and he frequently complained to Steven, "Who gives a fuck what year the war of 1812 ended anyway?"

To the frequently-asked question "Why am I doing this?" and the flood of additional negative comments that spewed from Henry's mouth on an almost daily basis, Steven just smiled and repeated, "Just keep your eyes focused on the goal. This is all about your earning a college degree."

Henry actually was doing that. He was really beginning to believe that he could really do this. As he lay on his bunk at night, waiting for sleep to overtake him, he was starting to believe that it really all could be his. Good job, fancy apartment, sexy girlfriend, a big income; it all seemed more and more possible *someday*.

In his daily routine inside Stillwater, money remained a constant problem. His days were busy with class and study hall, all at the miserly rate of 50¢ per hour. His former free time was now pretty much consumed with his time with Steven working on papers and reports. Maintaining his supplemental income required time too, time to make appointments and time to arrange the merchandise transactions, and time was now something Henry was always short of.

He was often able to arrange his one-to-one meetings with sexual customers during school hours by using the restrooms in the Education Building, but his merchandise transactions took a great deal of time to arrange, coordinate, and execute. That portion of his business resulted in a growing income stream, but it took the most time too.

A DEGREE FOR HENRY

By excusing himself from Steven to attend chapel several evenings each week, plus Saturday and some Sunday mornings, Henry was able to keep things moving along fairly well, but it took constant attention to make everything fit together.

One afternoon Steven returned to his room and found Henry's fancy watch thrown into the middle of his bunk. Steven knew that was a signal that Henry was in a fight somewhere. Henry had thrown his watch on Steven's bed in case he was caught and went to segregation for the fight. Henry's Seiko watch had once been legal for inmates, but under current rules, such fancy things from the outside were no longer allowed. If Henry went to SEG, they would find the watch and require that it be sent out or thrown away. Henry did not want to lose that swatch, a symbol of what a special fellow he was.

Just before afternoon count, Henry arrived at Steven's door with a grin on his face. "What happened?" Steven asked as he handed back the watch.

"Some new guy," Henry began. "He thought I was easy and called me a spic-fag. When I showed up in the showers, obviously prepared to do business, he became more polite. I think that he was hoping to join the PMBs, but he didn't realize just how high the dues were going to be. He ended up apologizing to me, and he gave me two Snickers bars to forget the whole thing."

The PMBs (Prison Motor Bike Gang) were a group of white men expounding Aryan beliefs of white power and domination. They kept mostly to themselves but were notorious for being a determined and dangerous group to anyone who crossed them in the prison's world. They were intolerant of anyone opposing their position and were known for having nothing to do with gays. Steven knew that Henry had been lucky, very lucky, but Henry's lifestyle and personality made contact and friction with the PMBs and with several other groups inside the prison inevitable. Most of all, Steven knew that he wasn't going to change Henry.

Steven also knew that Henry was playing with fire, and he reminded him, "You know," he began, "if you go to SEG, everything is down the drain. You'll lose the Spector assignment. You will be out of class and probably out of this unit. The degree and your chance for the good life on the outside, you'll flush it all down the drain."

"Yeah, yeah," Henry replied. "You keep telling me that. I know, I know, but no one can talk to me like that to my face. I've got to live in here, and no one is going to disrespect me like that. Besides, I knew the asshole was all talk. He'll just have to find another way to get into the PMBs. I would have hurt him bad, and he knew it."

CHARLES SLABAUGH

Steven briefly tried to explain to Henry that the Aryans, or bikers, as they preferred to be called, were a formidable, very close group that took care of themselves. He said that they should never be messed with; all to no avail. "They are all punks" was Henry's retort.

Steven replied that, "Those 'punks' could really hurt you," but Henry wasn't having any of it.

With that, Henry and Steven locked themselves into their respective cells for the afternoon count.

That evening, after supper, they went to work on a paper about the Polynesian people's trek across the Western Pacific Ocean. Later that night, as Steven lay on his bunk, waiting for sleep, he chuckled as he rethought the day's experiences. "This is a crazy existence, from an almost gang fight to a paper about the Polynesian people, all in the same afternoon."

To Steven, his effort to help Henry escape from his hopeless pit of poverty and ignorance was part of his life for almost nine years. He had come to prison from a small town, and he was serving a long thirty-year sentence as child molester. He and a teenaged daughter had become physically sexually involved. When his wife discovered what was happening, she called the police, and Steven's life had dissolved.

Arriving in MCF – St Cloud for intake, Steven had scored high in reading and math. When he arrived at Stillwater, he was recruited into the Education Department and ended up working for Jane Halverson's predecessor in Lit 1. When Jane arrived, he quickly became her lead tutor. His conviction had destroyed most of his lifetime friendships. While his mother and siblings stayed close, most old friendships evaporated when he pled "guilty" and was sentenced to thirty years. He hated prison but enjoyed teaching. Best of all, he was good at it, helping many find success and ultimately a better life.

Years before, he decided to help any students he encountered with the ability to do the work to earn their degree and find their way to what Steven knew was a possible world: a world of nice houses, good jobs, and clean, safe streets. If they were willing to try to do the work, Steven was very willing to help.

While he had certainly had his failures, he had two friends on the outside now with what he called normal lives. One of the friends was actually married, with a small growing family. Steven knew it was possible, and he was determined to try, but sometimes it was so very hard. The current project, Henry, was proving just how hard it could be.

Henry's midterm grades were better than Steven had hoped:

English Writing & Research	B-
History	C+
Anthropology	B-

But Henry was unhappy. "As hard as I've worked, I've sweat . . . I deserve all As," he complained.

Steven thought the grades were fair, but he didn't say so. There was no sense in creating another argument with Henry anyway. Steven was already planning ways to improve the grades in the semester's second half. Steven could see Henry was making progress and beginning to understand where they were going with these papers. Steven was beginning to see a glimmer of light at the end of the tunnel with his friend Henry.

Chapter 6

English Is a Big Problem

Jane had a new problem for me one morning. As she explained it, a new student in the class, an older Asian man who was, in fact, Hmong, had gone to segregation the previous night. His name was Shoua Lee, and I had not met him as he had only been in the class for a few days.

As Jane explained it, Shoua kept going to segregation for various reasons. Ignoring a direct order, being in an unauthorized area, and being out of his cell at the wrong time were but a few of the charges he had faced. In this case, Jane had gotten the unit lieutenant to understand that the problem was that Shoua didn't understand the commands that were being made. By assuring the lieutenant that she would fix the problem, Shoua was out of SEG and back in class. As she introduced us, Shoua greeted me with a smile about a mile wide and, in a very friendly way, quickly convinced me that he shouldn't be having all these problems inside Stillwater.

What had happened the previous night wasn't unusual at Stillwater. Shoua's unit was out of their cells enjoying flag privileges. Men were playing cards, exercising, doing laundry, and using the phones. This was a regularly-scheduled part of the men's day. Everything was completely normal and fine. Shoua was cooking noodles in a microwave oven. Suddenly, the PA system began announcing, "Switch in! Switch in!" In prison talk, that meant that everyone must immediately go to their cell and close the door. Unknown to Shoua, a fight had broken out in a cell on the other end of the unit and security was shutting down the unit as they prepared to quell the fight. This was also completely normal.

Most announcements at Stillwater came over the PA system. Because there were only a few speakers in each unit, and the units were quite large – almost a city

A DEGREE FOR HENRY

block long and four or five tiers high – the volume on the speakers was set very high.

Despite having been in the United States for almost ten years, Shoua often didn't understand what was being shouted over the PA. As everyone else quickly headed into their cells, Shoua quietly continued to cook noodles.

The C/Os in the unit's bubble observed Shoua standing at the microwave, seemingly ignoring the order, and he hit the alarm button, summoning the squad again, this time for Shoua. Not understanding what was going on or why he was the focus of the angry C/Os now in his face, Shoua was quickly handcuffed and was on his way to SEG. Had it not been for Jane and an understanding lieutenant, he could have easily been there for many days.

At Jane's direction, I started Shoua on a program of basic English, and I also got him started with our new Lit 1 phonics tutor. The news that we had a phonics tutor came as a surprise to me. We had never had anyone in that position before, but I soon met the new tutor: Henry Jiminez. Henry had managed to have himself excused from the Spector afternoon study hall two afternoons a week to become Jane's new part-time Lit 1 phonics tutor.

Steve Kline had helped make this happen for Henry, but it was news to me. Henry had told Steve that he had "more time than I need in study hall." This was true because he and Steve were spending so much of their free time working on Henry's papers and reports. I learned later that, for Henry, this was mostly a cover story. The truth was that Henry was dealing merchandise and that being in Lit 1 was the connection. Several men were selling their mental health drugs to a group of bikers. One of the men doing the selling was a Lit 1 tutor. He would bring the pills to class, and Henry would get them to a biker who worked upstairs in the library, which was on the first floor of the Education Building.

I never did understand how the biker's contribution, new sneakers, got to the African American in the kitchen next door who was supplying meat and cheese, but Henry controlled it all, and his getting into Lit 1 regularly was essential for the transaction to be completed. It was all part of getting Henry the income he so badly wanted, so Henry became a part-time Lit 1 tutor. In prison, the obvious answer doesn't always represent the whole story in many situations.

As the end of the semester approached, Henry, with Steven's almost daily assistance, was very busy preparing for course final exams and finishing his term papers. Henry's focus was on the final term papers, which he knew represented a large portion of his grade in each of the courses. While Steven was trying to get him ready for each course's final exam, Henry didn't believe that the final exam would be a problem. In Henry's mind, fitting together all the pieces of each paper so they told the entire story in concise words and still meet the instructor's guidelines for each project was like one of his intricately-constructed merchandise transactions. Each part of the puzzle had to fit into its correct place in the scheme, and each component had to be perfectly tailored into the scheme. To Henry, the final exam would be "not a problem for me."

Steven kept his concerns mostly to himself, but he knew how final exams often demanded that students recall small seemingly-inconsequential bits of information, so his desire for Henry was to go through a comprehensive review of everything in the three courses. To that idea, Henry just repeated, "The finals will not be a problem," and that is where the issue stayed, open and unresolved.

In the midst of doing his job as a tutor and helping Henry almost every day with is college work, Steven still tried to keep a personal schedule of things important to him. He always attended Sunday Catholic mass, and he also attended a weekly group that met in the main Stillwater religious activities area, the chapel. The meditation group met on Saturday mornings and practiced a version of transcendental meditation. It also served as a social outlet that Steven enjoyed very much.

At the moment, however, Steven's stomach was again very much on his mind. He was again having lots of acid reflux, and he was out of Zantac again. After a few days of sending kites and waiting for a reply, he finally received a pass to see Dr. Blumenthal, who renewed his prescription for Zantac. The doctor again said that he intended to send Steven to the hospital to get a look inside his esophagus. "I thought we were going to do that," Steven replied.

"We were," said the doctor, "but my boss overruled me. I just made out the request in again. We will get this done."

At Stillwater, when you were going out of the prison for any reason – to the hospital, to a court hearing, to see a doctor specialist in his office, or even to visit the funeral home upon the death of a close relative – you never had any notice of exactly when you were traveling. Some morning, as you returned from breakfast and were preparing to go to work, you would be paged to come to the unit's front desk. At the desk, you would be handed a pass to the Property Department or some other innocuous location. When you arrived at Property, you would be met by two C/Os who would take you to security. At security, you would be dressed in gaudy orange jumpsuit that proclaimed your status as an "offender"; your hands and feet would be chained and shackled so that you could barely walk upright.

A DEGREE FOR HENRY

Then you would shuffle out to a waiting car or van, and off you would go. Your work assignment at Stillwater and the entire system there would be advised that you were on "special duty," and everything was cool. Steven was anxious to make such a trip and learn why his acid reflux was getting so bad so often.

Finally, after much preparation, stress, and hard work, Henry's papers were finished and submitted, and all three final exams were taken. For over a week, he and Steven waited nervously for the results: the grades on each component and for the final course grades. When they finally arrived, both men were proved somewhat correct. Henry's papers were good, with the one in English Writing & Research being especially good and earning a grade of A-. Steven was right too; Henry's finals didn't go well. He got two Cs and a D+ in anthropology. Steven was devastated, fearing what the final course grades would be, but Henry took the news with a blend of anger and defiance.

"I knew this was going to happen," he ranted. "It's all bull, complete bull! Who cares how the Polynesian people divided their work between men and women? I sure don't. And I still don't give a fuck what year the war of 1812 ended! It's all dumb stuff and—"

Steven cut him off. "Henry, I know you're upset, but we've been through this too many times already. This is all part of a process to get you a college degree, an AA. I don't care how Polynesian people divided their work assignments either, but you need to, if you really want that good life once you're out of here. If all that you want to do once you get out is to quickly come back into prison, that's on you. I can't really help you unless you're ready and willing to listen to me, to do all the work and to learn this stuff. You need to learn all of it, not just the portion that you've decided that you like or that you think is important."

Their argument lurched on for three days until the final course grades were finally distributed. Henry's papers and generally good quiz scores carried the day, and his final course grades were

English Writing & Research	B
History	C+
Anthropology	C-

Steven was relieved but not Henry. His first reaction was "I deserved all As."

Steven smiled and said little. At least they were rolling now. With these grades, Henry wouldn't get on the honor roll, but he had passed everything, and Steven knew that things would get better. This was an acceptable start, especially when

CHARLES SLABAUGH

you considered Henry's complete lack of experience with this type of work. Steven felt encouraged and hopeful.

Henry immediately focused on the second semester, determined to get into the "computer stuff" that he considered essential to get a clerk's job in a Minncor shop.

The following week Henry met with Norma Kolkins to discuss his first semester's results. Norma told Henry that this was a good beginning, but she stressed that he needed to improve his grades in the coming semesters. Henry wanted to talk about which courses he would take next. Norma listened to his requests and concerns and told him that most of the group would take at least one computer course in the coming semester. She also told him that she had obtained the services of an excellent mathematics instructor and everyone would be taking a new course: Math for Liberal Arts. Norma said the instructor was a young man from Uganda who was a graduate student at the University of Minnesota. She described him as "an absolute genius at mathematics." It sounded okay to Henry. He was finally getting into computers.

His second semester courses were assigned the next week. As he looked at the list, all he saw was Introduction to Computers. The other courses were Health & Fitness and Math for Liberal Arts. To Henry, it all looked great, but Steven was concerned. In Henry's mind, Health & Fitness sounded easy, but Steven knew the course would dwell on food and nutrition and would amount to a lot of detailed bits of information. Henry was interpreting math as arithmetic, but Steven knew that the course would include algebra, geometry, trigonometry, and maybe some calculus; all subjects Henry knew nothing about. Steven was very concerned, but he said nothing.

In the ten days before classes got underway, there was no containing Henry's joy. He was most excited at the vista he saw unfolding before him. He could now really believe that the seemingly-unreachable goal of a college degree was possible. He dreamed of what that would lead to: a good job, maybe a choice of jobs; a good place to live; and finally, he would have enough money to live well, as he had always wanted to live. He was finally able to contemplate leaving prison as a truly good thing, a portal to the good life. More and more, Henry knew that the key to his finally getting the happy and successful life of his dreams – a life that had never been his, ever – was to get his college AA degree. In the short run, he knew that completing some of these courses would lead to a better job inside; if not a Minncor clerk's job, then another clerk's job inside the prison. Finally, it would all be his.

A DEGREE FOR HENRY

Finally, the semester began, and Henry met his teachers; all were new faces and personalities to him. He received his books, syllabus for each class, and the list of assignments. He made a beeline for Steven's room to show him the stuff. Steven had had a long day. Intense pain in his stomach had kept him up most of the previous night, and he had gone to sick call to see Dr. Blumenthal as he was again out of Zantac. He was lucky; the doctor was on duty at Stillwater that day, and he ordered the refill of Zantac. The pharmacy's location in Oklahoma would delay delivery of the medications for two or three days, but at least they were coming. Steven didn't like what Dr. Blumenthal was telling him. With a smile and a firm voice, the doctor said to Steven, "They turned us down again, on the trip to the hospital, but I'm going to send in the request again today. I want to see what's going on down there."

As Steven was already feeling pain in his midsection, he asked if there was any way he could get some Zantac that day. The doctor said "no," but he assured Steven that he would put a rush on the refill order.

All that and a growing pain in his stomach were on Steven's mind as Henry was telling him about his day and his expectations for the new semester. Pulling his attention back to the moment, Steven smiled and agreed that it was going to be a good term. He picked up the math book and flipped to the table of contents. As he feared, the book seemed to begin with algebra, assuming that the reader/student had at least a basic knowledge of Algebra. From there, it went on through geometry, back to advanced algebra, and then on to trig and calculus.

Steven understood basic algebra, the kind taught to GED students, but this course went way past Steven's knowledge. Actually, Steven could see that the course started beyond his understanding of the subject and then went on to a very high level that he had never explored. He tried to show Henry what lay in front of them, but Henry was not in the mood to be discouraged. He knew that he was on his way to success. In Henry's mind, without a doubt, he was on his way to a great life. Once he was rolling with a hot car and a fancy apartment, he'd also get himself a sexy girlfriend. He thought to himself that night as he lay on his bunk, "Hell, I don't even prefer girls, but what the hell, I might as well have it all. Then even these assholes who have always put me down will know that I have it all."

The next morning, as Shoua Lee and I were laboring through an English story book, Steven dropped by the table and asked, "How are you with algebra?"

"Fair," I replied quickly.

I'd taken the basic course in seventh or eighth grade, but Math was never a big part of my life. Just then, Jane announced that the class was going up to the library. I wanted to take Shoua up there, hoping to find a book on his native land, Laos. Our trip to the library ended my conversation with Steven, although I wondered why he was asking about algebra.

Later that evening, after supper, I asked Steven about it, and he explained his concern for his friend Henry and the college math course. Steven said he was going to look for another helper for Henry on the math course as he didn't think it was his cup of tea.

Henry was constantly doing things for no reason, except for show. His merchandise business had been pretty good, and that morning he had bought a shirt and pants from another inmate who needed money. That inmate had just purchased the clothing from the JCPenny catalog with money his mother had sent in. Now he needed money to cover a loss from a fantasy football bet, and he offered the clothing to Henry for half price.

In those days, Stillwater inmates were allowed one civilian shirt and pants for wear only in the visiting room. Henry, who hadn't had a visit in several years, now had three civilian shirts and two sets of pants. It was all part of Henry's determination to always have better clothes, shoes, etc., than anyone else. It was all about his compulsion to be a special man in this one-size-fits-all environment or anywhere else that he found himself. What Henry didn't want anyone to know was that he hadn't had a visit in years and didn't expect one soon. Owning fancy clothing that he couldn't even wear was just for show inside the prison. Henry desperately wanted everyone to think that he was special.

A few days later, a new tutor joined the Stillwater literacy effort. Douglas Sorenson was an older guy who was a lawyer in real life. Doug was doing a long bit as a repeat sexual offender. He was new to Stillwater and quickly found work in the Education Department. Possessing a college degree and a law degree, he was, by far, the best-educated man – staff, student, or tutor – in the entire department. As a sexual offender, he was destined for a tough life in prison, something he already knew from his previous prison sentence.

Sexual offenders were known as cho-mos, prison slang for child molesters. They were labeled by all, shunned by many, and under a constant and real threat from some. Cho-mos were sometimes attacked for no apparent reason, and they quickly learned to never relax or to drop their guard. Some men refused to speak with them; others would refuse to sit next to them in class or in the dining room. Without exception, they could never relax in prison. With a perpetual smile on

A DEGREE FOR HENRY

his face, Doug Sorenson spoke to everyone and seemed confident that his superior intelligence and welcoming ways could surmount any obstacle that his return to the world inside of prison would present.

Steven quickly approached Doug, inquiring about his math skills. Doug said that he could teach algebra and had done so at St. Cloud. He said that he had also taken trig and calculus. Steven quickly explained the problem to Doug, who, just as quickly, said, "Sure, I'll be glad to help Henry."

Now Steven had to get Henry on board. He knew the reality of Doug's crime as a sex offender was a huge potential problem with Henry, but he saw Doug as the solution to a potential obstacle to Henry's goal of earning a degree. Steven had to first present what he saw as a huge problem looming in Henry's future, the Math for Liberal Arts course, and what he saw as Henry's complete lack of preparation for it, complicated by Steven's lack of math expertise. When Steven presented what he saw as an absolute windfall, Douglas Sorenson, Henry's reaction was immediate: "No fucking way!" he shouted. "That fucking cho-mo is just a piece of crap. Are you nuts? I have a tough enough time getting respect in here. I don't need to be tied to that fucking cho-mo. No way!"

Steven immediately stopped talking. He knew Henry well, and he knew that there was absolutely no hope of changing his mind when it was so firmly made up on a subject with such emotional connotations. "Well, I'll just have to figure out a different way," Steven mused as he recoiled from Henry's angry outburst.

Steven often said that it was a miracle that he and Henry were friends as Steven himself had an SO case. What made it different was that Steven's case was with an almost-grown daughter and Doug Sorenson's cases were always with very young children. In Henry's mind, the age of the victim made a huge difference; plus, Steven's situation was completely mutual. There was, of course, a third factor: Steven helped Henry get things that he wanted.

If Henry's outburst to Steven didn't seal the matter in concrete, it was made officially dead later when Henry and Doug came together face-to-face down on B West's flag. Henry was doing laundry when Doug came walking by. Always cordial to all, Doug came right over with his hand out and a broad smile on his face. "Hell-o," he began. "I'm Doug Sorenson, and I hear you need some help with math."

Henry cut him off. "No, I don't need a thing from you, you cho-mo motherfucker. I'm fine. You just need to stay away from me, or there's going to be a big problem in your lousy life."

CHARLES SLABAUGH

Doug Sorenson was new to Stillwater, but he knew this drill from a previous bit in prison. Without a word, he dropped his hand, his face frozen in a smile. Then Doug walked away, not looking back at Henry. From experience, he knew he now needed to avoid any and all contact with Henry. Watching the entire encounter from the rail in front of his cell high up on the third tier, Steven Kline thought, "I hope Henry has a good plan for getting through Math for Liberal Arts because he just threw a great plan out of the window."

Once the semester got underway, Steven's friend Henry jumped into his three new courses with vigor. The computer course was his major interest, and he knew it was critical to his getting a better job inside Stillwater. It took a great deal of concentration, but he was having fun. As Steven predicted, the Health & Fitness course put great emphasis on food and nutrition and also on healthy lifestyles. Henry was bored with it, frequently telling Steve what a complete waste of time it was. Steven kept reminding him that it represented another two hours of the degree program's 64-credit-hour requirement.

From day 1, Math for Liberal Arts was a problem. Henry didn't understand algebra, and he liked it even less. From the first day, his comment was "Who gives a fuck what the value of X is?"

Steven tried to point out that X is just a concept. The idea Steven kept saying was to learn how to solve a problem when we didn't know all the numbers. Even when Steven would attempt to demonstrate a practical situation where algebra could be used for finding the solution, Henry would listen, but he was very quick to dismiss the whole issue. When the course work advanced to higher levels, and Henry didn't understand the basics, his confusion and frustration grew.

With Steven's assistance, Henry got through the daily and weekly homework assignments in Math for Liberal Arts. When Steven asked how the weekly quizzes were going, Henry would answer okay but would offer no specifics. Steven had noted that the syllabus specified a midterm exam and then a final exam. Of concern to Steven, each of those exams constituted 35 percent of the course's final grade.

Taking care of what he could, Steven encouraged Henry to begin preparing for his paper and final exam in Health & Fitness. Steven felt that he could really help Henry with that course. Thankfully, the Intro to Computers course required no paper or weekly quizzes. The entire course grade was to come from a series of projects, all done in class on the computer. Steven was off the hook with that course.

Chapter 7

Reading Is Fundamental

Early in my second year working in Lit 1, Jane motioned me over to her desk as we all arrived for work one Monday morning. "We're getting a new student this morning that has some special needs. He's got some health issues, and one of them is diabetes. It has affected his eyesight, or at least that's the fear. I want you to work with him."

I said, "Okay."

As the students arrived fifteen minutes later, two of them were new faces to me, and one of them ultimately arrived at my table. My other morning student, a young Mexican named Felipe, was leaving prison on Thursday, so I wasn't surprised to be meeting a new student that day. Jane quickly introduced me to Bernard Diamond. Diamond was a big black man of maybe 6 feet in height and easily 325 pounds. He had an easy smile and a firm grip as we shook hands and greeted each other.

As was my habit, I first tried to get acquainted as he sat down to my right. Jane had mentioned that he had a problem with his sight. I was surprised that he was not wearing eyeglasses but then noticed a pair of state-issued black plastic-framed spectacles riding in his shirt pocket. In response to my question where he was from, he answered, "South Minneapolis, but I grew up in Chicago."

Chicago was a city I had once known pretty well, so I asked, "What part of Chicago, Southside, Westside?"

His answer, "Cabrini Green," came quickly and told me a lot.

CHARLES SLABAUGH

Cabrini Green had been a huge public housing project in LBJ's war on poverty that had started with much promise and didn't end well. In the end, the government demolished it when they completely failed at controlling crime and the degradation that its name came to symbolize in the Windy City. I was pretty sure that Bernard's life had been tough.

I went on to explain our program to Bernard, telling him that Lit 1 was mostly a reading program. When men improved their reading skills, they would move on to one of the other literacy classes, and ultimately, they would tackle the GED tests. Bernard's only comment was that "I won't be here long then. My reading isn't a problem."

Before he had arrived, Jane had shared Bernard's reading and math scores from the testing he had taken at MCF – St. Cloud. Bernard's reading score was pretty low: second grade. I didn't get into that but went on to give him a tour of the room, pointing out the several computer rooms, the several sets of encyclopedias, and the substantial collection of books on many subjects. The books were really helpful, written on adult subjects but written at lower reading levels. Our guys trying to learn to read didn't have to try to find interest in traditional children's books.

With that, Jane called the roll and introduced our two new students: Bernard and a young Hmong inmate to the class. Before we got into anything, I asked Bernard one more question. "Everyone calls me Chuck. How would you like to be called?"

Many of the men were very fussy about how they were addressed, and I always asked that question, trying to make them comfortable. "I'm Bernard or Mr. Diamond, I don't go for that nickname crap" came his reply.

"Since we're going to spend a lot of time together, I'll stick with Bernard, and like I say, I'm Chuck to everyone here."

He nodded in agreement, and I grabbed a book on shipping on the Great Lakes, written at a third-grade level, saying, "Let's give this book a try. It's about shipping on the Great Lakes. Did you ever see any of the big boats on Lake Michigan when you lived in Chicago?"

"We never went down to the lake, and I can't swim anyhow" was Bernard's reply.

It immediately became obvious that Bernard's statement that reading wasn't a problem wasn't correct. The reality was that Bernard couldn't read. Even common, basic words, like *it*, *is*, *on*, and *or*, were a big problem. Trying to suggest a fix for

A DEGREE FOR HENRY

his trouble, I offered, "I see that you're not wearing your glasses, Bernard. Why not try it with them on?"

He answered, "Oh, I forgot that I had them with me today, but I really don't like to use them. They're so ugly."

I had to agree, the glasses the prison supplied were unattractive in the extreme. Made of heavy black plastic construction, the frames looked like 1950s style to me. To most inmates, they were a sure sign that the wearer lacked money. Inmates with money available ordered glasses from outside the prison, using catalogs that showed current styles. Poor inmates were forced to use the state-supplied glasses or, as many chose to, to do without.

When Bernard tried the book again with his glasses on, the results were better but only marginally so. It seemed to me that his second-grade reading score was about right. "Now what to do next?" I wondered.

We had many men with low reading skills in Lit 1; sometimes we could help them progress, all too often we could not. When I had first joined the class, I was amazed that in our high-tech world, there really were people who couldn't read, but that was often the reality in Lit 1.

In the weeks that followed, Bernard and I pursued several different strategies in trying to raise his reading level. We tried many different books from Lit 1's mini-library. It was soon obvious that he liked books about cars and auto racing. "Did you have a car?" I asked one day.

To that question, Bernard said, "No, my daddy had one once, but it got wrecked."

When I asked if he had liked school, he said that he had seldom gone to school. "Man," he said, "I lived in Cabrini Green. We didn't go to no school. We was out hustlin'!"

In time, he spoke of his father who could seldom find work; a sister Bernard described as a crack whore; another sister who had lost both legs, the victim of diabetes that ran rampant through his family; an elder brother in the Minneapolis suburb of Crystal; another brother recently dead of a drug overdose in a Kentucky prison; and a loving mother who was a great cook.

Weeks turned into months, and our objective of raising his reading level remained unfulfilled. He did his best, but the combination of poor eyesight, which was compounded by his tendency to forget to bring his glasses to school and his

CHARLES SLABAUGH

apparent inability to retain most of what he was exposed to in class, left us accomplishing little.

The stated objective of the Lit 1 program was to teach our charges to read, but Jane also firmly believed in helping them learn what she called life skills. For some, that goal evolved into something as simple and basic as getting used to showing up for class every day. For others, it might involve learning how to keep track of a running balance in a bank account, while others would try to plan a month's financial budget.

As Bernard and I wrestled with his almost-total inability to read, we explored many alternatives and options to working with traditional texts and ideas about how people learned. Phonics was an option that Jane had advocated earlier, but we quickly discarded it. Bernard had no idea which letters made which sounds. Worse, he plainly didn't care, and his memory issues seemed to prevent him from remembering what he was shown or had just seen. He became very angry and frustrated when he failed at coming with the right answer or sound, and we moved on.

In an attempt to hone in on areas of interest, I kept trying to find out what he liked to do, but it seemed that he had few interests. As far as I could tell, he had almost no interest in sports. His size and substantial affliction with diabetes made playing sports difficult, and unlike many of Stillwater's inmates, Bernard seemed to have no interest in even following sports. When I asked him what he liked to do, he answered, "Talk to my family on the phone, but I can't do that anymore." When I asked why, he explained that his parents now lived in Gary, Indiana, having exchanged Chicago's inner city blight for Indiana's nearby clone. In either case, it cost an inmate about 40¢ a minute or $6 for a fifteen-minute phone call to phone anywhere outside of the Twin Cities metro area. With Bernard's two-week paycheck, totaling maybe $15, I knew the price was prohibitive.

"Maybe you could save up for a call?" was my suggestion.

"Save up!" he said. "Save up what? I don't get any money. I have nothing to save up with. I get a damn indigent bag every week but no money. I have nothing to save up with. I trade stuff in the bag for chips or a candy bar or whatever."

His angry answer confused me. All students were paid 50¢ an hour for school, so he was earning about $7.50 a week for his fifteen hours, half time school schedule. If men owed a fine or owed a court-ordered restitution, or if they were trying to accumulate a gate fee, the system took half of their pay for that purpose with the inmate getting the other half to meet his personal needs.

A DEGREE FOR HENRY

The gate fee was cash for the inmate's needs upon his release on parole. At that time, it was $100, but the amount was later raised to $500. The idea was to ensure that every man had at least some money in his pocket when he left prison. To accumulate that money, half of any and all earnings were deducted for the gate fee account once an inmate was assigned to any prison job or school assignment.

"Bernard, how can you have no money? None of us have much money, but everyone with a job or school assignment gets some. If there is something wrong with your pay, we need to tell Jane so she can get it fixed."

With that, Bernard sighed and told me the whole story. Several months before, something had plugged up the toilet in his cell. Bernard said that he didn't know what had happened, but he suddenly had a stopped-up toilet. This was not an unusual problem with around 1,250 men using plumbing that was from sixty to ninety years old. When Bernard reported the stoppage to a C/O, the inmate twenty-four-hour emergency plumber was quickly dispatched to Bernard's cell with a snake tool.

The twenty-four-hour emergency plumber quickly cleaned out the pipe, bringing up a torn black do-rag and three old inmate socks. Bernard quickly denied putting the obstructions in the toilet, but as he had been the only occupant of that cell for several months, the system quickly blamed him for the blockage. A few days later, Bernard's mail delivery brought him the notice from inmate (offender) accounts, telling him that his account had been charged $132 for repairing the "damage to your toilet." As this situation had been ruled an act of abuse of state property, inmate accounts would now take 100 percent of any money flowing into Bernard's account until the entire $132 was paid. Bernard quickly went on to tell me that the inmate twenty-four-hour emergency plumber probably earned only 25¢ per hour (the pay rate for that job was published as 25¢-$1 per hour, depending how long the inmate had been in the assignment), and the entire episode took only a few minutes to clear. In Bernard's mind, the entire matter was yet another example of "the man" ripping off the little guy. When I tried to raise the question of how the old do-rag and the socks had gotten into the toilet, Bernard again denied responsibility and said that wasn't the point anyway. I stuck with that idea a bit longer, assuring Bernard that I wasn't trying to be his enemy, but that I really wanted to understand what had happened. Finally, he said, "I was mad. My brother Jerome had died in prison in Kentucky. Jerome had been on heroin for all his life, and he got some bad prison-made stuff or took too much of it, and the night before, a C/O had stopped at my door to tell me to call home, that someone had died. I didn't have any money on my phonebooks, and I told him so. He said that he couldn't help me and walked away. I didn't know who had died. He just said that I needed to call home because someone had died. I finally got a buddy to spot me a local call to my other brother who lives in Crystal. My brother told me that our other brother, Jerome, had OD'd in the Kentucky prison. He also told me that my momma was having trouble with her diabetes too, but he didn't know how bad off she was. I was damn mad."

I said, "Why didn't you ask to see your case worker? They can and do help with calls like that and—"

He quickly cut me off. "That's just crap! My case worker is some bitch who just sits in her office drinking coffee. Every time I see her, she tells me to get to work and finish my GED so I can get a real job. That's all I ever get from her, more BS about school." He then asked me if Jane could help him make a call because he needed to check with home to see how his momma was doing.

I told him, "No."

Just then, Jane announced that the students were leaving and our day in school was over.

That night I had a minor brain storm, and I brought several kite forms to class the next day. When Bernard arrived in class the next morning with the student group, I explained my plan. With my help, Bernard was going to write a kite to Chaplain Gilbertson, explaining that he had zero money and a sick mother in Gary, Indiana. He was going to ask the chaplain to arrange a phone call to his mother. Bernard liked the idea of the free call home but quickly doubted his ability to produce an acceptable kite.

Writing the kite became our first lesson for the morning, actually for that morning and most of the next morning too. First, I explained what needed to be said. Bernard kept asking if this would work and why the chaplain would care. "I don't go to church much," he kept repeating.

I assured him that while Chaplain Gilbertson would certainly enjoy seeing him in chapel anytime, that wasn't the issue. When I suggested we try to write it all out on a blank piece of scrap paper first to practice, Bernard clearly preferred to begin using the proper yellow kite form. As I had brought only a few kite forms to class, I insisted that we begin with the practice concept. We went through many practice versions of the plea, frequently having trouble with grammar, punctuation, and with Bernard's challenging handwriting. By the end of the morning, we had produced one version that I found fairly acceptable. Bernard was unhappy that we didn't have a version finished, but I assured him that we could easily finish the project the next morning. It was probably good that we had run out of time; Bernard was clearly exhausted and stressed, his face shinning with sweat.

The next morning, on our fourth attempt, we got an acceptable kite written. I cautioned Bernard to handle the kite with care as he carried it back to his unit for mailing in the living unit mail drop. Bernard promised to immediately mail the kite when he arrived back in A East, and I crossed my fingers. The next morning, in class, he happily reported the successful completion of his mission. "Now when will he call me down?"

Bernard was now consumed with apprehension and curiosity. I had no idea when Father Gilbertson would send for him, but I thought he did things like that on Saturday mornings, and I suggested that as a possibility. I told Bernard that I had no idea how long he could talk, but I assured him that the father would charge him nothing. At my reference to the "father," Bernard said, "Father? I thought you said that he was the chaplain! Why would he help me? I'm not even Catholic."

After I explained that the man who was Stillwater's chaplain was also a Catholic priest and that he served all, Catholics, Muslims, and even those who believed in nothing, Bernard seemed okay, but he still mumbled, "I'm not even Catholic."

The following Monday morning it seemed to take forever for the student group to arrive in the class, but when Bernard came through the door, his smile seemed to light up the entire room. From 40 feet away, he flashed me a big thumbs-up sign. When he sat down, he immediately began talking: "I talked to my momma for a long time. My sister answered the phone and told me that Momma was in the hospital. She has been in the hospital for a long time – several weeks. Her diabetes has been very bad. My sister didn't have the hospital's phone number, but she knew the hospital's name. The chaplain called someone else and got the number. You were right, Chuck, he's a nice guy. He didn't even look like a father. Anyway, my momma sounded real good. Daddy was there with her. They have been worried about me since I haven't been calling. My Auntie Bert was there too, and I got to talk with her too. The chaplain – what's his name?"

"Chaplain Gilbertson," I filled in.

"Yeah, well, he said that he would send me a pass again next Saturday, and I can call her again. I sure am glad we sent him that kite. That was a great idea. It sure was great talking with Momma and Daddy."

Bernard went on for the next few minutes, telling me of the call. His smile dimmed only slightly when I suggested that we needed to get to work, but with no argument or complaint, Bernard opened his *Target Spelling* book, and we again attacked the issue of his reading problems.

A week later, on Monday morning, Bernard reported another pass from Chaplain Gilbertson and another conversation with his family. This time they had found his mother at home. He was very glad to know that she was better. In class, Bernard's reading wasn't much better, but his attitude showed vast improvement. There was no doubt that he was happier and his outlook was more positive in general.

A few days later, Bernard brought a new notice from inmate accounts. This notice was the standard one reporting that $132 had been received on his account. Less the mandatory 10 percent DOC deduction on most incoming funds, this advised Bernard that $118.80 had been credited to his account on that day. Bernard's account had carried a negative balance of $67.12, which now left him with a balance of $51.68 to the good. I read the notice which showed "God's Truth Church" as the remitter. I explained the notice to Bernard and asked him, "Do you belong to God's Truth Church?"

For a minute, he looked very confused, and then he smiled. "Do you remember I told you that when I called my momma, she was in the hospital and my Auntie Bert was visiting her? Well, Auntie Bert is my momma's sister. She is a big wheel and longtime member of God's Truth Church in Gary, Indiana. She must have got them to send me the money to pay my plumber's bill. I already paid some of it. How much money do I got?"

I went over the math again.

The next morning Bernard showed up in class with his weekly Canteen order form. The Canteen was where we bought everything. In 2003, the Minnesota Department of Corrections had closed the individual Canteens that each individual prison ran and substituted a new, combined program run by Minncor. The stated purpose was presented to us was to lower prices via volume buying. To the DOC and the Minnesota Legislature, the objective was to create enough additional income for Minncor to put their books in the black. For many, many years, the legislature had to inject money into Minncor to balance their books, and the legislature had said, "Enough is enough," demanding that Minncor operate as a profitable business. Giving Minncor the DOC's Canteen operation had created several hundred thousand dollars of additional income, and the Minncor account turned black.

The centralized Minncor Canteen offered over six hundred products, from basic hygiene items to clothing, to over-the-counter medications, to candy and food

A DEGREE FOR HENRY

items. If you had money on your books, you could order once a week from the Canteen.

"Chuck, can you help me with this? I need to get it right. I need lots of stuff."

Completing the weekly Canteen order form was a big problem for many of the Lit 1 students, and often students asked their tutor for help. I quickly agreed. At the top of the form, the inmate had to fill in his name, OID number, his unit number, his cell number, and then fill in his OID number again, this time on a bubble grid. As each man was given only one copy of the Canteen order form, I did the bubble grid for Bernard.

I then asked him, "Have you thought of what you'll need in hygiene stuff?" Bernard looked at me curiously, so I went on. "Now that your toilet bill is paid, you will begin to receive your pay again, and they will no longer give you indigent bags, so I am wondering if you need soap, shampoo, deodorant, laundry soap, or any of that kind of stuff . . ."

"You mean I won't get that stuff free anymore?" came Bernard's quick response. "That's okay," he went on. "I've got lots of that stuff. I want to order six Swiss rolls, six honey buns, six Snickers bars, and—"

I cut him off. "Bernard, this is your money. You can do with it as you choose, but have you ever considered trying to go a little slower and making it last for a bit?"

On my mind, but unspoken, was the thought of a badly overweight diabetic loading up with enticing snacks, loaded with sugar and calories, not being the smartest purchase for Bernard to be making.

We bantered the idea of not spending all the money immediately around, and Bernard agreed to ordering smaller quantities of several of the sugar-intensive items, all the while insisting that he had lots of toothpaste, soap, etc. The order we ended up with totaled about $27, leaving almost half of his windfall unspent. As I reflected on the episode later that evening, I was pleased that he had exercised at least some restraint with his order.

When the Canteen order day arrived a week later, Bernard didn't bring his order form to class as I had hoped he would do. Curious, I asked, "Did you remember that we order Canteen tonight?"

"Yeah, I remembered that, but I don't have any money."

"How's that?" I replied. "You should have $24 or so, or at least I think so, Bernard."

"No, we added some stuff to my order last week when I got back to the unit" was his reply.

Apparently, a buddy had helped Bernard rework last week's order back in the unit. *So much for financial management*, I thought to myself, but I said nothing.

A few days later, Bernard and I were in one of the Lit 1 individual computer rooms. We could use those rooms for quiet and privacy, allowing the students to use a series of reading, phonics, and some math programs that Jane had provided via CDs. We were finishing a phonics program and Bernard mentioned wanting to know more about the nation of Islam. Surprised, I said, "We probably have information on that in an encyclopedia program, but I thought you were a Christian?"

"I am," he quickly replied. "But I've been hearing that Elijah Mohammed was such a great man. I would like to know more about him."

"Give me a minute," I said, and I walked over to the Lit 1 clerk, Pauly Dassel, turning in the phonics CD and asking for a new CD package for the *Encarta Encyclopedia*.

In a few more minutes, I had it in our computer, and Bernard and I were scanning its menu for information on the nation of Islam. With my reading from the screen, Bernard seemed fascinated with the story of Elijah Mohammed and the nation of Islam that he had mostly created. To my complete amazement, Bernard seemed to be following what I was reading, and he seemed truly interested in the flow of information. We finished the morning that way, with me reading to Bernard and him listening intently.

When the student's day was over, I approached Jane with an idea. Before he had left the classroom, Bernard had thanked me and asked if we could do that again. "There's a lot of stuff I'd like to know about" was the way he had put it.

I put it simply to Jane, up to this point, I'd made almost-zero progress with Bernard in my attempts to improve his reading skills. Part of the blame might rest with his eyesight problems or with his diabetes or with his cardiac problems, but the underlying problem was that he really wasn't interested. Now he had expressed interest or at least curiosity in something or in a process. My question to her was "Could Bernard and I begin spending part of every day doing similar research via the electronic encyclopedia? Further, could I print out excerpts from the

A DEGREE FOR HENRY

encyclopedia of things Bernard found of interest? As you know, in addition to his basic reading deficiency, Bernard finds it almost impossible to read from a computer's screen."

Without hesitation, Jane agreed. "Sure, if he's interested, give it a try, but if his interest begins to fade, we'll have to move on and try something else."

The next day I reserved an hour in one of the computer rooms, and at the appointed time, I told Bernard we were going in there. We had used the computer before for spelling programs and for a math exercise. Bernard hadn't liked either. His eyes were a real problem when trying to read from a computer screen, and he immediately told me that he didn't like the computers. I smiled and said, "We're going to try something new. If you don't like it, or if it doesn't seem productive, we won't do it again."

Once we were in the room, alone and in front of the computer, with me at the keyboard, I told him that we were going to look for information. I then asked him what he would like to know more about. After a moment's hesitation, he said, "My momma always said that Franklin Roosevelt was a great man who helped our people, but I don't know why she said that. Did Roosevelt free the slaves?"

I said, "Okay, that's a good place to begin. Let's find out why your mother thought he was so special."

Fortunately, the *Encarta Encyclopedia* had a huge file on FDR, and for the next hour, we explored. The computer screen was mostly a blur for Bernard, but with me reading, we covered a lot of ground. From the Great Depression to the new deal and through World War II, we skimmed over all of it. Bernard was like a kid with a new toy. His questions came a mile a minute. He was especially interested in Roosevelt's efforts to help black people, and Bernard was surprised at Mrs. Roosevelt's work to help blacks also. When the tutor with the next reservation for the room rapped on the door at our hour's end, we were surprised that the time had passed so quickly.

When we returned to our table, I walked over to Pauly Dassel at the clerk's desk, and he handed me a sheet of paper. Bringing them back to Bernard, I said, "I've printed out some of the Roosevelt stuff we just found, plus a file we found on Elijah Mohammed and the nation of Islam. I thought you might want to work on them here too."

The almost-instant delight in Bernard's face was amazing. "Do you mean that I can have these?" he gasped.

CHARLES SLABAUGH

"Yes, Jane says we can do this if we use them to help your reading" was my reply.

He was as happy as any kid on Christmas morning.

In the days that followed, Bernard used the files on Roosevelt and the nation of Islam daily, trying to read and understand them. On the following Monday, he arrived in class with a vinyl-covered three-ring binder he had purchased at the Canteen. The binder took me by surprise. They were sold to inmates to store personal pictures in, but Bernard told me that this new one was for his "research."

Taking a clue from that, Pauly Dassel and I conspired to print out a cover sheet titled "Bernard's Research," which we glued on the cover of the binder. When I showed Bernard his now-personalized binder, Bernard's pleasure was immense and total. No child on Christmas morning was more delighted than Bernard was at that moment.

After the students left for lunch, I brought Jane up-to-date on our experiment. She was pleased and said that she would tell Bernard how happy she was the next morning at class. That next morning, she approached our table and gave Bernard the ultimate Lit 1 "pat on the back." She told him, "Since you are doing so well and working so hard, as of Monday, you will become a full-time student, coming to class mornings and afternoons. Keep working so hard and you'll make enough progress to earn your GED."

Bernard was so surprised, he could only manage a "yes, ma'am" before Jane was off on her next mission around the room. After she left, Bernard asked, "Does that mean that my pay will go up?"

I assured him that his pay would double, assuming that the class met for all scheduled periods. To a Lit student at Stillwater, that was very good news indeed.

I then asked Bernard what other subjects he wanted to research. His answer surprised me somewhat, but we made a list: Harold Washington, Chicago's first black mayor; Stevie Wonder, the famous performer; and Florence Nightingale, the world pioneer nurse. Also on his list was Social Security. "Did Lincoln create that?" was his question.

We made a study plan, and we agreed that we would spend an hour every morning on the computer researching. As I had another afternoon student who needed my time too, Bernard would spend most of the afternoon learning to read the printed out files on our research. We could already tell that the printouts were proving easier for him to read than the computer's screen.

A DEGREE FOR HENRY

Slowly, Bernard began making progress with his reading. We only tested Lit students quarterly, but even before his next date for testing arrived, we were sure we could see evidence of real progress. He seemed to have fewer problems with the smaller words that had once been hard for him to comprehend, and in general, he had fewer problems and many more good questions.

As I watched him read, I noticed that his face was always very close to the paper, even when he was wearing his glasses. He hated the ugly state-issue glasses, as did all the men forced to wear them, but he finally had admitted the he could really see better with them. When I asked how old his glasses were, he said that they were very old. "From the last time I was in prison."

"You hung on to them when you were out?" I asked.

"Yeah, I needed them for work, and I couldn't afford a new pair" was his candid response.

I mentioned this and my observation that he did not seem to be seeing all that well with them to Jane. She said, "Why doesn't he put in a kite to the eye doctor, asking for an examination?"

"He's done that, but the wait is running twelve weeks or more" was my answer.

Jane said, "Oh, we'll see," with a small smile.

After I left her desk, she went into her back office. I saw her consult a prison staff phone directory, and then she made a call. In three days, Bernard had a pass to health services to see the eye doctor, and in about ten more days, Bernard had a new bifocal version of the ugly state eyeglasses. It took him a while to get used to the bifocals, but he quickly reported that he could see better.

The new glasses and Bernard's increased interest in his schoolwork were slowly beginning to improve his reading skills. While he still found the concept of sounding words out an insurmountable task, there was no doubt that he was reading better, much better. We still had almost two months to go until the next scheduled reading test, and Jane and I were quite sure that his next test scores would show improvement. Hardly a day passed that Bernard didn't come to school wearing a wide smile and bringing a new subject that he wanted to research. We would talk about the request, and if it seemed possible, he would add it to the list he was keeping in his binder.

CHARLES SLABAUGH

I had learned that this was Bernard's third time in prison. He had been convicted of assault, and then the Minnesota Three Strikes Law (career criminals) law had been applied to his case, giving him a virtual life sentence. The Minnesota Public Defender's Office had taken on his case, successfully arguing that the career criminals law had been misapplied to his situation.

That law required that all three convictions be for the same offense, and that was not the case with Bernard. His convictions were probably caused by a lifelong addiction to heroin, but they were, in fact, for different felonies. He had served time for possession of drugs, burglary, and now assault, but he had not met the requirements of the law. The court took thirteen years off his sentence. He was still doing a lot of time, almost seven years, but that was a great deal better than life.

Suddenly, one Thursday morning the students arrived in Lit 1, but Bernard wasn't with them. When Jane called his name as she checked the roll and he didn't respond, she looked hard at his empty chair and then at me with a questioning stare. I didn't know what to think. Bernard had turned into a dream student, I couldn't imagine what to think. *Maybe he's ill?* my mind considered.

As soon as the roll call was completed and the day was underway, Jane went into her back office and got on her computer. In a few minutes, she came to my table. "He's being transferred to Faribault (MCF – Faribault) right now as we speak." She seemed unhappy. "He was reclassified for medium custody, and Faribault must have had an open bed. I'll have a new student for you tomorrow."

With that, she returned to her desk.

There wasn't anything to say. He was gone. We could hope he would do well in his new location, but regardless of that, he was gone. Inside the prison system, there is seldom an opportunity to say goodbye, and there was always a new man in the wings.

The new man was a very young Mexican: Raphael Garza. As Jane introduced us, I was struck by his youthful looks and by his extensive collection of body art. He had obviously been in prison for a long time, and the prison tattoo artists had been very busy. His arms, hands, fingers, and neck well adorned with various images that ranged from a cross on his left forearm to a pattern on his neck that proclaimed him a member of the Latino gang The Latin Kings. A huge depiction of a girl, fully naked on his right arm, was colorful and anatomically impossible. He also had teardrops on his one cheek and his thin white T-shirt revealed more prison art on his chest and back.

After Jane finished her introduction and left us, I began asking him what he would like to be called. "My friends call me Chuckie, but you can call me Garza. I won't be here long anyway."

"Are you going someplace?" I asked.

"Probably to the hole" was his reply. "I never do well in school anyway. School's all bull, and I don't like it much."

"Do you prefer time in SEG? There really isn't much to do there," I asked.

"How do you know?" came his quick reply. Before I could answer, he went on, "It's all a bunch of bull anyhow. When I get out, they will send me back to Mexico. What good will a gringo GED do me there? I've been to prison for eight years already. I know all about school. It's all bullshit."

Taking any opening I could find, I asked, "Eight years? Were you ten years old when you came to prison?"

That made him almost laugh. "I was fifteen years old when they sent me to Red Wing (MCF – Red Wing). I was there for four years, then they sent me to Appleton (Appleton was a private prison in Appleton, Minnesota), then to St. Cloud, and then to Faribault, and now here. It's all bull!"

"You were in medium custody, and now you're in close custody. You're going in the wrong direction," I commented.

"Yeah." He again smiled. "They think I'm a badass. Wherever they send me, just because I'm small, some asshole always assumes that I'm easy. Let me assure you, I'm not easy."

With that, Garza crossed his arms on his chest and slid down in the chair.

As I looked at him, I knew this was going to be a tough sell if I was ever going to get him interested in school.

In the weeks that followed, I learned a lot about Garza. He was twenty-three with a brother doing life at St. Cloud. He had been in the USA since age two, when his parents brought their four sons illegally across the border into California. The family lived there for a few years until the parents split up. Garza's dad took the eldest boy with him to Colorado, and his mom brought her three younger boys with her to join two brothers in St. Paul's East Side barrio. Garza was the third

CHARLES SLABAUGH

child, the second son was in St. Cloud, and the youngest son was still home with their mom. Garza said, "Every Sunday morning, Mom brings my younger brother here, and they visit me. Then they drive to St. Cloud and visit my brother there, and then they drive home. My brother says Mom cries all the way home every Sunday." Garza shared his concern for his youngest brother, the one still at home with their mother. "He's already in the gang. I'm afraid he will end up in here."

Garza was, at best, an indifferent student. Having grown up in a bilingual world, he spoke English and Spanish, but he was really neither the master of either language. In school, he spoke English, often confusing or misusing pronouns and verbs. With his Mexican The Latin Kings gang buddies, he spoke Spanish. I was trying to learn some Spanish myself, but my halting Spanish was quickly overwhelmed when Garza and his buddies spoke very fast and seemed to run words together. I quickly got frustrated and confused, and then I tried to just follow their animated conversations.

With me in school, he was open and frank in his disdain for being forced to go to school and for being forced into the GED process, to his frequent lament, "When my time is up, I'm going to be deported. What good will a Yankee GED do me in Mexico?"

I had only a weak, uncertain rebuttal that hoped a bilingual Mexican could find a better job inside Mexico than one who spoke only Spanish; a relatively-poor Spanish at that. His friends told me that Garza's English was better than his Spanish. He came to class only because he had to avoid being locked in his cell as an unemployed inmate. The money was of some incentive, but Garza's heart definitely wasn't in his school program. He was bright, with a quick mind, but he categorically refused to take anything we were doing seriously. He was bored, and I was frustrated.

Garza told me that he didn't mind the time he spent in segregation. He said that he filled his nights talking with friends, and when he was awake in the afternoons, he wrote poetry in Spanish. When Jane posted a notice about a creative writing contest sponsored by the Minnesota literacy council, I had an idea. Like many young men in prison, the only public notice Garza had ever received in his life was when he had done bad things. How would he respond to some positive notice, I wondered.

The next day I brought a copy of the notice over to the table and made him aware of the contest. The contest was an annual affair with all entries found acceptable to be printed in a book at its conclusion. To be included in the book was the prize. His first reaction was "I can't do that!"

A DEGREE FOR HENRY

He folded his arms over his stomach and put an angry look on his face.

"Why not?" I asked. "I thought you said that you wrote good stuff."

He quickly took the bait. "I do write good stuff, but it's all in Spanish. Will they consider work in Spanish?"

"No," I told him. "They are all about English, but why can't you write a poem in Spanish, and then I'll help you translate it into English?"

After some banter, he liked that angle. I think the real attraction was the chance to get away from our drills of spelling and grammar exercises, but he did agree, and we were soon hard at work on the contest.

An initial problem came with his tendency to use profanity in his poems and to use graphic sexual topics. I explained that to be seriously considered, the language and the images depicted had to merit a G rating. He tried to argue about that as a creative issue.

"You're denying me the right to be creative . . ."

I finally said, "Look, this is their contest, and we're pretty much stuck with their rules. If you are really creative, we can tell your story using their rules."

He finally agreed, although insisting that they were just being "chicken shit." With his cooperation being closer than I had ever thought possible, I let his final criticism lay unmolested, and we got to it.

In a very little time, he had written a poem in Spanish. The translating took us several days, but it was finally completed. I typed the poem up on a computer word processor, and after final edits, we presented it to a somewhat surprised Jane. In an earlier part of her life, Jane had lived in South America, and she was fluent in Spanish. She went over both versions, and with surprisingly few additional changes, she pronounced the translation acceptable and agreed to submit it to the Minnesota literacy council's contest.

The next morning Garza came to class wondering if he had "won." For a moment, I didn't understand the question, but then I realized that the contest was his concern. I reminded him that the contest was for an entire month and was statewide. I told him that the literacy council's book would come out in sixty days or so. "Damn" was his reply. "I've got some business coming up, and I hoped to know about this before that goes down."

CHARLES SLABAUGH

Confused, I asked, "What business? What's going down?"

To my question, Garza became very vague and quiet. Sensing that I was entering very dangerous ground, I suggested that we get down to work, and he glumly agreed.

The next morning Garza didn't show up for class. When the roll call was ended, I asked Jane about my missing student. She said, "He is in segregation, and I don't know anything about it."

Knowing that Jane always checked her e-mail the first thing every morning and that she read every incident report for the entire prison every morning, I suspected that she knew a great deal more than she wanted to share with an inmate, but I didn't press the matter.

Later that day I heard that Garza had been involved in a fight, a big fight. Actually, it was more of a "hit" on behalf of his gang, The Latin Kings. They had assaulted another gang's member, and five guys were in SEG; all of them facing lots of time as the man they had attacked was in the hospital in serious condition. Now I understood about the business Garza had said was coming down.

Two months later, the Minnesota literacy council's book came out with Garza's poem prominently printed inside. At that point, he was still in SEG, and I asked Jane if she would get him a copy of the book. "No," she quickly replied. "That's his loss for acting like an animal."

I didn't respond. I knew Jane pretty well, and when her mind was made up, there was no changing it.

Six or seven months later, on a Monday morning, two new students arrived in class. As they stood in front of Jane's desk, I recognized one of them as my old student Bernard Diamond. Jane first dispensed with the first man who was disputing a very low reading score. That score was the reason he had been assigned to Lit 1. "I ain't no dummy," he told Jane twice. She retired to her back office and used the phone. A few minutes later, she handed the unhappy fellow a pass. I heard her say, "It's upstairs on the main floor across the library. We're lucky, Mr. Marcus has time to retest you right now. We will have this confusion cleared up by lunchtime."

The inmate, looking no less unhappy, headed up to the testing room, and Jane turned her gaze to Bernard Diamond.

A DEGREE FOR HENRY

"Hell-o, Bernard. It's nice to see you again. I heard that Faribault didn't go well. Are you ready to give this another try?"

"I guess so," Bernard mumbled. "Will Chuck be my tutor?"

Jane glanced in my direction. "Probably not," she began. "Chuck has two morning students already. He would have little time to give you . . ."

"That's not a problem, I'll take whatever time he can give me. Chuck and I really got along. I'd really like to be with him."

Jane said, "Wait here for a moment, Bernard," and she motioned me to her back office, where she closed the door.

When the door was shut, she said, "You're in high demand this morning. I don't want to bury you. What do you think? You and Bernard did work well together."

"Does Bernard have to come in the morning?" was the way I started to answer her. "I'd have more time in the afternoon."

Jane said, "The morning session lasts thirty-five minutes longer than does the afternoon period. I'd like Bernard to be in class for as long as possible. I can put him with another tutor, but he's right, you two were good together."

Surprising myself with the boldness of the question, I asked, "Why is he back from Faribault?"

"He got in a fight. He assaulted a young guy he didn't even know. He was in segregation for ninety days."

From Jane, that was quite a lot of information.

"Okay," I said, "I'll take him. Miller, my one morning guy, goes home in three weeks anyway. We'll make it work."

We scrounged a chair for Bernard, and he seated himself next to me at what was now an extremely-full table. When you considered that the concept of Lit 1 at Stillwater was a one-to-one student-tutor ratio, we were way out of balance, but we all got acquainted and got to work.

In our first direct conversation, Bernard asked if we could get back to researching subjects on the computer. He volunteered, "I've still got my research binder. Should I bring it to class tomorrow?"

95

CHARLES SLABAUGH

"Sure," I told him. "You may bring it down, but I doubt we'll be able to jump on a computer right away. With three students, I need to be here at the table for most of the period."

Two days later, one student didn't show up for class, and another had a health services pass for the dentist. As it was just Bernard and I, I signed up for an hour in a computer room. When the time for the reservation arrived, we moved into the room with the *Encarta Encyclopedia* program in hand. Bernard had several subjects on his list from before. As I was navigating to the first subject, Charles Lindberg, I asked Bernard, "What happened in Faribault? I hoped you would do well down there."

"Faribault was okay," he began, "but school was bad. I couldn't do fun things like this in their school. All they would let me do was workbook after workbook. I got tired of that."

"Okay," I said. "But I heard there was a fight. Did someone mess with you?"

Bernard smiled. "Nah, no one messed with me . . . ahh . . ."

Bernard was at a loss for words, something unusual for him.

Sensing his discomfort, I said, "Bernard, forget it. It's none of my business anyway. I was just surprised to hear that you were in a fight. I never saw you as a fighter."

Bernard said, "To tell you the truth, it was all about the phones."

He paused, and I asked, "The phones?"

He began again, "Well, here, I could phone my brother Monte. He lives in Crystal with his girlfriend. The call was cheap, 37¢ for fifteen minutes. Even as broke as I always am, I could do that once or twice a week. From Faribault, that call cost me over $6 for the same damn call! I couldn't afford it. I only make about $7 every two weeks. I was real mad that I couldn't call my brother and his girlfriend anymore. So I started that fight just to get sent back here. I didn't even know the guy. He was just some little white punk who was walking toward me one day on the way to breakfast. I never would have done it if I had known how much SEG time I was going to get for it. I figured I'd get a week or ten days and then come back here, but they gave me 180, do 90 days because I really hurt him. That was his fault. If he had just fallen down, it would have been over with, but he fought back. He hit me hard, and that really made me mad. It was his fault."

A DEGREE FOR HENRY

By now, Bernard's face was flushed, and he was talking very loud.

Speaking very softly, I said, "Bernard, you started a fight with some guy you didn't even know for absolutely no reason, and because he fought back defending himself, you say it's his fault! That makes no sense, my friend, no sense at all."

"Sure it does," Bernard retorted indignantly. "If he had just quit, it would have been over, and I wouldn't have had to hurt him, and I would have been back here two months ago. Now it's even more messed up. I used my last phone call to my brother Saturday after I got here. He and his girlfriend split up, and my brother moved out. His ex-girlfriend accepted the call just so she could tell me what an asshole she thinks my brother is. That spent my last phone call, and I didn't get any family news. I asked her what was going on with my momma and daddy, and she said that she didn't know or care, and then she hung up. Can you beat that? I always thought she was a nice gal, but I can tell why my brother moved out. She's a real bitch. To me, this is all the fault of that asshole in Faribault fighting back. He really messed me up."

We got through the morning, but we really accomplished little. Bernard was upset over his lack of phone money and information about his family. I was unable to shake what I thought was Bernard's strange logic from my mind, so we pretty much just went through the motions of doing something all morning. Finally, thankfully, Jane announced the end of the period and dismissed the students to go to lunch.

In the remaining twenty or so minutes of my working morning, I printed a copy of a crossword puzzle I had made up for an afternoon student and went over to the desk of the class clerk, Pauly Dassel, to pick it up. Pauly was a good guy. Serving a long sentence, he had made a good niche for himself in the Lit 1 classroom and was of considerable assistance to many tutors as we worked with our many varied students.

As he handed me the puzzle, Pauly said, "I see you got Bernard back as a student. How did that go?"

"I'm not sure," I answered.

Then I told him about Bernard's fight story and Bernard's conclusion that it was all the fault of the poor, nameless Faribault inmate. When I finished the story, Pauly said, "Yeah, I can relate to that absolutely. This is my second bit inside, and I absolutely know how he feels."

CHARLES SLABAUGH

With a sinking feeling in my stomach, I stammered, "How's that?"

"It's kind of a long story," Pauly began. "I was finishing my first bit at Stillwater. I'd been there almost three years. I'd done all the mandated classes, treatment, and I'd taken all the programs they required: anger management, critical thinking, focus on the family, plus six month's CD (chemical dependency) treatment. But I knew that I wasn't really ready to go out. About three weeks before my SRD, I went to my case manager and told her that I wasn't ready to go out. Her answer was, 'When your time is up, you have to go out.' I talked to C/Os and my unit lieutenant, and the answer was the same, 'When it's your SRD, you leave. There is nothing we can do about it.' So the day came. They gave me my gate money and sent me out. It's a long story, but in three weeks, I was locked up again, this time with an assault/murder charge. I've been here for nine years, including some time at Oak Park Heights, and I've got sixteen more years to do. It's all the fault of that crew that was here then and wouldn't listen to me. If they had just let me stay here for a bit more, it all could have been avoided. At least that's how I see it."

With that, Pauly turned to help another tutor who was now standing next to me. I took my puzzle back to my table.

The next morning Bernard came back to class with the student group. When I saw him, I could tell something was wrong: He just didn't look right. He looked glum, depressed, and his usual smile was missing. Concerned, I asked how he was doing. "Not worth a shit" came his reply. "I must have eaten something bad last night. I didn't sleep worth a shit. I kept waking up, and breakfast this morning didn't taste good to me. My guess is that the cook messed up something."

"Maybe you should go on sick call?" I ventured.

"Nah" came his reply. "I need to be here, I'm so broke, and I need to get with Momma on the phone. For that, I need money, so I've got to stay in class, and sick call costs $3. I can't waste the money."

For a few minutes, I tried to convince Bernard that he should go to Jane and say that he was sick, but he would have none of it. He insisted that he was fine, and besides, he needed the money. As he was staying, we got to work.

We spent the first hour at the table. Thinking that it might lift his mood, I had signed up for an hour on a computer in the midmorning. When the time for our appointment arrived, I said, "Why don't we do some research for an hour or so?"

A DEGREE FOR HENRY

I was anticipating some excitement from Bernard, but he just said, "Okay," and that was it.

As we moved into the computer room, Bernard was moving very slowly, and he dropped into the room's chair with an audible sigh. "You okay?" I asked.

"Yeah, like I said, I didn't sleep worth a shit last night." Then after a pause, he asked, "What are we going to research today, Chuck?"

"The next thing on your list is NFL football. What did you want to know about it?" was my answer.

"Oh yeah, I wanted to know who owns the NFL? That sucker must be a rich dude. Can we figure that out?"

For the next fifteen or twenty minutes, we looked at the encyclopedia's file on the NFL. As was our system, I read the screen, and Bernard asked questions, except today Bernard was very quiet. When I read that one of the NFL's founders was George Hallas - the legendary founder of Chicago's Bears team was Bernard's favorite - I expected a positive comment from Bernard, but he was silent, and he was perspiring heavily. "Bernard, are you all right?" I asked.

He was slouched way down in his chair, looking at the floor, when he replied, "No, my chest hurts, and I feel like I'm going to throw up."

"Stay where you are. If you get sick, try to use the waste can," I said as I quickly went to Jane's desk.

Interrupting her conversation with another tutor, I said, "Something is wrong with Bernard. He's got chest pains, and he feels sick, and he's sweating a lot."

Without hesitation, Jane punched the button on her belt-mounted radio, triggering an "A level" emergency alarm. I heard the screech for an "A level medical" go out over the air.

The system immediately told Control whose radio had sent the alarm and exactly where inside Stillwater that radio was located. In seconds, Control asked Jane for confirmation. Like a pro, Jane answered, giving her name and saying that "an offender is having chest pains."

I was surprised that Jane knew how to talk on the radio.

CHARLES SLABAUGH

It was a poor joke among inmates that the A team of the squad ran to A levels for staff members and walked to A levels for inmates, but very quickly, the A team arrived in Lit 1, followed by two nurses pushing a wheelchair. As the nurses huddled around Bernard in the small computer room, the sergeant from the A team reported on his radio that an offender was being treated in Lit 1 and that he, Sergeant Patterson, was in command.

Bernard looked terrible. He was dripping with sweat, and he was way down in his chair. The nurses took his temperature, pulse, and blood pressure. The sticker on his ID identified him as being an insulin-dependent diabetic, and via her radio, one of the nurses confirmed that he had received his insulin at the morning's pill run. Getting Bernard moving from the chair where he was sitting and onto the wheelchair was complicated by the room's small size, his substantial size, and the room's congestion and narrow doorway, but finally, he was ready. As they began to push him out of the room, the A team sergeant advised Control, "The offender is being transported to health services."

As they wheeled Bernard past me, he smiled and gave me a weak wave of his right arm.

That was the last time I ever saw Bernard Diamond. Later we learned that in addition to his problems with diabetes and obesity, Bernard was now diagnosed with congestive heart failure.

Most men with that many health problems would end up in MCF – Faribault in a unit named Linden, which was set up to deal with health issues. Unfortunately, for Bernard, MCF – Faribault is a medium-security prison. Thanks to his recent fight there, Bernard was now classified close custody. Faribault was not an option. The last I knew, Bernard had been sent to the infirmary at MCF – Oak Park Heights, a nearby supermax. The staff there was trying to stabilize his condition and induce him to go on a diet.

Chapter 8

Doug Has a Bad Day

The fourth week in the new semester for the college program, an event in B West captured everyone's attention. Doug Sorenson had, by chance, ended up living on B West's third tier, in the back not far from Steve, Henry, and me. After his verbal blow off by Henry, Doug pretty well kept his distance from Henry, but Steve and I saw him often. With his friendly, outgoing manner, he was, as far as I was concerned, a welcome addition to the neighborhood.

Doug had become a real asset to the literacy program, doing tutoring in math in the Lit 3 and Lit 4 classrooms. With an easy, comfortable style, he was accepted by most of the students and was able to help several of them understand numbers.

One morning at breakfast, Doug had finished his meal, and as was the practice, he was taking his dirty tray to where we inmates set such things in a rack. When the rack became full, a kitchen worker, another inmate, would push the rack of dirty trays back into the kitchen to the dishwashing machine. The worker would then exchange the rack full of dirty trays for an empty rack and push the empty rack back to the dining room where it would be refilled.

As Doug walked by several tables full of inmates, one young white inmate with a beard and a shaved head slapped Doug's middle section and said, "Stay away from me, cho-mo!"

The young man had been hoping to do this for several days. He didn't know Doug, but he knew of him as an infamous cho-mo. This morning was the first time Doug had walked right by him. The young man, Nathan Osborne, was new in prison and very new to Stillwater. Nathan's cousin, Samuel (Sammy) Dent, was a PMB.

101

CHARLES SLABAUGH

The PMBs were a gang of white men advocating white power in the extreme. They sought power, wanting to be in charge of as much of the daily life at Stillwater as they could. Nathan very badly wanted to join the PMBs. In Nathan's mind, being a PMB was cool and most desirable. The PMBs were his new buddies. He worked out with them in the gym, hung out with them in the yard, and he longed to become a member.

When he asked his cousin, Sammy, about becoming a member, Sammy said that was a fine idea. He said, "You're doing the right stuff; you don't hang out with any niggers, spics, or ragheads (meaning Arabs of which there were none at Stillwater anyway), and most of all, you don't hang out with any cho-mos. I'll check with the president and get back with you."

The next afternoon Sammy came back to Nathan with the answer. "To earn your bones with us," as he put it, "you need to get that asshole cho-mo Doug Sorenson into a fight, and then you need to beat him up badly. You'll end up in the hole - but not for long - and then you'll be one of us."

Nathan smiled. "No problem" was his reply.

Like many PMBs, Nathan instinctively disliked Doug Sorenson. First of all, he was a cho-mo, someone who hurt kids. Second, he was a suck-ass tutor, working in education, teaching those stupid niggers and spics to read and count. Third, and maybe most important to Nathan, Doug Sorenson was a lawyer. Everyone in Stillwater had a horror story about lawyers who had screwed them by charging too much or by talking them into a plea deal the inmate now regretted or some any other variety of reasons that led the inmate to being in prison while the lawyer was now having lunch at the country club at the inmate's expense.

Nathan's slap to Doug's midsection that morning was designed to provoke the desired fight. What Nathan didn't know was that long ago Douglas Sorenson had contemplated a situation just like this one. Knowing that prisons throw both sides in any fight into segregation immediately, and that both sides in almost all fights end up doing substantial SEG time, Doug promised himself not to be goaded into any fights. The fact that he wasn't any good with his fists had helped him adhere to this decision. Doug was 100 percent nonconfrontational in his life at Stillwater, using a smile to quickly disengage from any potentially-dangerous situation. Doug was also very careful with whom he spends time, and he spent a lot of his free time alone in his cell.

In this case, Sorenson, who was fifty-three years old, was facing a muscular young man in his early twenties, which did nothing but reinforce the decision not to fight

A DEGREE FOR HENRY

with him. Doug had always said that he would report any assault or incident that threatened him, and that is exactly what he did immediately.

Without missing a step, he walked over to one of the many C/Os standing at the front of the room and said, "I was just hit and yelled at."

He then pointed out Nathan Osborne who was standing up with his fists clenched and with an angry look on his face. Nathan hadn't anticipated this and thought, *No real man would do such a thing.*

The C/O Doug Sorenson had approached with his complaint immediately hit he alarm button on his belt radio, and the squad's A team came running. The dining room was an area of extreme concern at Stillwater. Over five hundred inmates filled its seats during meal times, and at least ten C/Os were in attendance at all times. The fear was that a two-man altercation could easily erupt into a riot, so any alarm in the dining room brought an immediate and big response. Unknown to Nathan, to engage in a fight or to attempt to start a fight in the dining room often resulted in a charge of "inciting to riot," which could carry a SEG sentence of 180 days. All that Nathan knew right then was that the situation was not going well as four members of the squad's A team were closing in on him. He was quickly in handcuffs and on his way to the security center as was Douglas Sorenson. This was SOP for the A team. They made no decisions as to what was right or wrong. Everyone involved was assumed to be in the wrong, and all were handcuffed and taken to the security center. The staff there would sort it all out with help from the C/Os who witnessed the incident and by running back the film from the dining room's many cameras.

By supper that night, Doug Sorenson was back in his cell, having spent the entire day in a holding cell, eating a miserable bologna sandwich and a half pint of milk for lunch. When it was confirmed that he had done nothing, at about 3:45 PM, Sorenson was released and sent back to B West just in time for the 4:15 PM count.

Not so for Nathan Osborne. When the two C/Os in the security center began questioning him, he spouted off what a "miserable cho-mo prick Doug Sorenson is." Nathan's rant went on for several minutes and clearly established who the antagonist was. To Nathan's dismay, his own words revealed the hatred he felt for Sorenson and clearly established who had started the incident.

As the sergeant explained to Nathan, "You attempted an assault in the dining hall. You have clearly shown that this is a hate crime, which makes this a very big deal. Normally, you'd get 180 days for the assault in the dining room and 90 more because it was a hate crime, making 270 days total, but—"

103

CHARLES SLABAUGH

Nathan cut him off mid-sentence, "270 days just for hitting that cho-mo motherfucker!"

The sergeant continued, "You'd do better today if you would just keep your mouth shut. This is a very big deal, and I'm trying to help you. Your SRD is in 217 days. I'd rather not go through the paperwork of extending your SRD, but I can. It's all up to you. Here's my offer: If you will agree to the 217 days in SEG, I'll just leave it at that. You'll be in SEG until your release. If you don't want to do that, to agree to the charge and the sentence, we'll go for a new, outside, formal charge in Washington County District Court for assault as a hate crime, and we'll ask for three years. The choice is yours."

Nathan was almost numb; he was so upset. He hadn't known how seriously fights in the chow hall were viewed. He had assumed that he would get thirty days, do fifteen, not 270 days or, God Forbid, another three more years in prison. *All for that fucking cho-mo*, he thought.

Doug Sorenson's snitching was the talk of the prison that night as we went through the evening's routine. Doug was very pleased. Sure the day in the security center's holding cell was no fun, but he was relieved to know that his long-planned strategy had worked. Like all men with sex crimes in prison, he was always worried about the very real possibility of an assault. Now he was convinced that his plan to report any and all problems immediately was the right decision.

A few days later at school, my star student, Omar Oogolala, failed to come to class. To miss school because of illness was one thing; although even for a genuine illness, you didn't want to fail to report for work too often. Somehow I didn't think Omar was really sick. The students were allowed to "lay in" one day a month, but only for one day. On a hunch, I went up to the library using a pass I obtained from Jane. My friend, Dale Bishop, was working for the inmate newspaper, *The Prison Mirror*, and the paper's office was in the library.

After pretending to look for a book for a few minutes, I walked over to Dale's desk and asked about Omar. Dale immediately looked very sad as he started to talk. "As you know, Omar is from Sudan. One brother got to Minnesota with him. That brother is in St. Paul. Their mother and three sisters are in a UN refugee camp in Ethiopia. Omar has heard nothing from his mother or from his sisters for over two years, and the last news he had heard was that his eldest sister was very ill. The camp has a first-aid facility but no doctor. If someone becomes very ill in those camps, there is no one to help them beyond treating symptoms. To make matters worse, Omar has stopped hearing from his brother in St. Paul. He doesn't know why, but his brother has stopped visiting or even answering Omar's calls. Omar

A DEGREE FOR HENRY

is frantic with worry. Omar has almost no money. Omar's income is about $32 a month. He gets that only because he is enrolled in a program from the Mental Health Department for those with special needs. He attends Lit 1 as a student, but he doesn't receive the normal student pay of 50¢ an hour. The mental health money is his sole income. He has to cover all his personal needs, from hygiene products to laundry soap. Plus, paying for any phone calls and postage needs had to come out of that. With any remaining money, he can purchase food items and snacks from the Canteen. With a small bottle of Tide detergent going for over $6, his income doesn't stretch very far. Somehow he saved enough money to call a pay phone number he had inside the Ethiopian refugee camp. All telephone calls are expensive for inmates, but international calls are extremely costly. A fifteen-minute call to Ethiopia costs $27. On Sunday, Omar had enough money on his phone account to cover such a call, and he dialed Ethiopia. The first two times, no one answered. The third time, someone answered. They could not help Omar. He was very depressed and didn't sleep well."

Dale knew Omar from church, the soccer field, and they both lived in the same unit, A West. As a long-serving inmate, he knew how serious it would be if Omar missed another day of school, and he promised to do his best to get him there the following day. Omar was in Lit 1 because he needed help with his English but also as part of his being in the special needs mental health group.

When I returned to Lit 1, I shared the story with Jane. Without hesitation, Jane promised to not make a big deal of Omar's absence today if he made it to class tomorrow.

That night in B West, I saw Steve Kline and Henry Jiminez working in Steve's cell. Later that night, Steve confided in me his concern about Henry's college work. "I know we can get through the Health & Fitness class okay, and I'm not really involved with the computer class – that's 100 percent in the classroom – but I'm very nervous about the math class. It must be a very tough course, and the instructor, some African guy from the University of Minnesota, is very hard to speak with. His answer to any problem seems to be, 'You need to study and work harder,' but Henry insists that it's okay and that he is fine. That sounds good, but I know that Henry is completely over his head with math, especially with this math."

I didn't have much to offer, and Steve and I went on to other topics, but I was very curious. In my heart, I hoped that Henry would successfully get through the course, but my mind kept telling me how extremely unlikely that hope was.

CHARLES SLABAUGH

The next morning Omar Oogolala came to school, and true to her promise, Jane didn't mention the previous day's unexcused absence. Omar was present in body, but he was obviously preoccupied. When I asked him about his call to Ethiopia, he said it hadn't worked and added, "I am worried about my sister. I have heard nothing from her for a very long time. The number I called is a public phone at the building where those in charge work. I thought maybe someone smart would answer and know some news. That did not happen. The person who answered didn't know them. It's okay, but that was a lot of money - $27 is a lot of money." Then he asked, "Will you pray for my sister?"

I told him that I would pray for her and also for his mother and for him too. With that, Omar opened his English spelling workbook and went to work.

After work, I stopped at Steve Kline's door. He was kneeling in front of his toilet, obviously being sick. His stomach was not doing well. Later I saw Henry enter Steve's cell with his Health & Fitness book. Steve and I didn't get to visit that night before we were locked down.

The next morning in Lit 1 was working with my newest student Shoua Lee. His grasp of English wasn't improving, but his friendly, cooperative way and his mile-wide smile was always a delight. Midmorning, we began a phonics drill with our new phonics specialist, Henry Jiminez.

Henry had gotten Jane to hire him part time to do phonics tutoring. At first, he was in class only two afternoons per week, but this semester's school schedule gave him two open mornings also, and Jane had agreed that he could work those mornings also. Shoua was cooperative as always, but phonics seemed to confuse him. In his free time, Shoua was trying to learn to write his native Hmong language, something few native Hmongs could do. This written version of Hmong was a recent creation of scholars in the West. It was written using the English alphabet, but the phonics was completely different. Shoua was having an awful time keeping it all straight in his mind.

When Shoua made repeated errors in speaking an English sentence, Henry erupted, "No, no! Why can't you gooks get this right? It's so damn easy, if you just try!"

Henry was angry. Shoua was confused. I was like Henry, very angry. I had seen Henry erupt like this before. His anger was usually directed at a member of a minority group, usually someone like Shoua who was older or someone Henry perceived as weak. In a similar situation I knew of, an incident like this resulted

A DEGREE FOR HENRY

in a fight back in the lower level of the Education Building's restroom, when an older Cuban inmate wouldn't accept Henry's bullying.

In this case, I quickly jumped in, telling Shoua that we'd return to our regular work/study area and go over the lesson again. Henry interrupted me, "But we're not done!"

"Yes, we are," I countered. "We're all done."

Shoua and I finished the morning at our usual table, and Henry sulked in the corner at a computer work station. After the students left for lunch, I approached Jane carefully.

Mindful of the constant prison rule to never snitch on another inmate, I was determined to be careful of what I said, but I was determined to remove Shoua from Henry's angry words. Actually, it was easier than I imagined. "Jane," I began, "Shoua is making some small progress with phonics, but the sessions with Henry are not working. Shoua just isn't ready for the concept, and he is growing confused. I'd like to stop his sessions with Henry while I work with him on the basics of phonics, one to one."

"Is there a problem?" was Jane's reply.

"No," I lied. "He's just not ready yet."

An "okay" from Jane ended the meeting, and I took the decision to Henry. Henry didn't like it when I told him, suspecting that I had revealed his attitude problems to Jane. I assured him that I had not, that it was just a case of Shoua not being ready for phonics.

As we ended our conversation, Henry offered, "Okay, too many of you tutors are way too easy with these gooks. They just can't learn."

For the moment, I left it there and smiled as I headed back to my table. Then halfway back to my table, I just couldn't keep my mouth shut. Returning to Henry, I said, "For what it's worth, Shoua speaks four languages: Hmong, Lao, Thai, and some Vietnamese. And now he's learning English. How many languages do you speak, Henry?"

With that, I turned away, and with Henry looking at me with an angry, puzzled look on his face. He finally shouted, "Whatever!" and picked up a book from his table.

Chapter 9

Mayhem

One night after supper, I was doing my laundry and watching bits of an old John Wayne movie between trips down to check on the machine's progress with my load. Doing laundry that way could be hazardous in B West. We had only five pairs of washers and dryers to service about 260 of us, so getting a machine could be problematic, especially in the evening when almost everyone was off work and back in the unit.

Sometimes, if the machine you were using ended its cycle and shut off with you not standing right there when the light on the machine went dark, the next guy in line might remove your clothes to make room for his load, and you could lose track of your stuff. If you lost your state-issued T-shirts, blue long-sleeved shirts, jeans, shorts, or socks, you were in trouble. You could only get one issue every year, and the Property Department kept very good track of who was due for a new state-issue and the exact dates they were eligible. If you did lose things, or if they wore out too soon, you could get a pass to visit what we still called the laundry (still called that despite the fact that the laundry function had long ago left Stillwater) and pick out replacements from a bin of used clothing that was kept there. The clothing in this bin was from men leaving Stillwater for parole. When men left on parole, they took the clothing on their backs. The rest of their state-issue was laundered and put in these bins. Some of it was in fair shape, some of it wasn't.

For that reason, wise inmates never got too far away from their washing machine or dryer. A worse problem sometimes came when you were laundering your sweat outfits or the gray T-shirts, items purchased from the Canteen and which most of us wore when we were not at our jobs. The sweats were more comfortable and were a bit of a status symbol. They were all made by Minncor, and they were gray,

A DEGREE FOR HENRY

but having them somewhat separated you from the men with no money. As such, they were prone to disappear when left lying around, and some were stolen when left unattended in washing machines or dryers.

As my stuff was rinsing, I noticed that I had forgotten to put a dryer sheet in my pocket for the dryer. Taking my bottle of laundry soap with me (leaving that lying around loose was also an invitation to trouble), I climbed the two flights of stairs to the third tier and walked down to my room, which was in the middle of the tier. As I was returning the bottle of detergent to the shelf and grabbing a dryer sheet from the box, I heard something bang into metal with a loud clang. The sound repeated itself two or three more times, and I became curious about what was making the noise. I went out onto the tier. Two cells to my right, Dale Sorenson came running out of his cell two doors down from mine. Turning to the right away from me, he ran for the back stairs that led down to the flag.

Sorenson was a mess. His face was bloody, his glasses were missing, his blue long-sleeved shirt was half torn off, and he was obviously frantic to get away. I will never forget the look of absolute terror and desperation that was etched on Doug Sorenson's face at that instant. Behind him, Sammy Dent emerged, fists clenched and a grim, determined look on his face. Sammy immediately began to chase after Sorenson, chasing him down the tier and around the corner to the entrance to the stairs going down.

Suddenly, I heard the clapping of many hands and loud cheering. Looking down to the flag, I saw thirty or forty inmates standing and cheering. They were watching the chase, cheering and clapping their hands as Sammy Dent, hoping to strike a few more blows, chased Doug Sorenson. I heard the alarm sounding from several C/Os' radios, and the C/O on duty at the back of the flag began shouting "Stop that!" over and over.

Usually, when a fight occurred in a cellblock, the entire unit would be quickly locked down while the C/Os figured out what had happened, and the blood cleanup team was summoned to deal with the mess. Not wanting to lose my clothing in the ensuing confusion, I walked left to the cellblock's middle double stairway and went down, avoiding the fight's aftermath as I worked my way to the laundry machines in the back of the unit near the showers.

When I got there, I found my clothes on spin, and I waited for the machine to conclude its cycle. As I stood there, the squad arrived, and the appreciative audience had stopped cheering and clapping. All were trying to assume a casual posture along the building's outer wall as they awaited the show's next act.

CHARLES SLABAUGH

They didn't have long to wait. A bloodied and completely-disheveled Doug Sorenson soon emerged, coming down the steep steel stairs; his hands handcuffed behind his back. His eyes were already forming dark circles. His nose was bloody, smashed in, and crooked. Blood was all over what was left of his shirt; and he was visibly unsteady on his feet. A C/O from the squad held his elbow, steadying him as he negotiated the stairs.

When he got to the flag, he and the squad members escorting him turned left and headed for the B West front door, maybe a city block ahead of them. An anonymous voice from high up on the tier shouted, "Cho-mo, prick!"

When two C/Os from the squad immediately moved to the flag's center, looking up, trying to locate the sound's source, no further insults were heard.

In a moment, Sammy Dent emerged from the stairs, also handcuffed with a C/O on each side, but Sammy had few signs of any altercation. His clothes were not mussed, his white T-shirt was bloodied with what I assumed was Doug's blood. Sammy had a big smile on his face and a defiant grin. A cheer erupted from several onlookers on the flag who had been hugging the wall's shadows, and two or three men began to clap. An angry shout from the A team's sergeant, "Stop that!" brought the cheers to a quick end.

As we all stood there watching, both groups moved to the unit's front door and off to the security center.

By now, my washer had finished its cycle, and no order to switch in had been sounded. As a dryer was empty and waiting, I quickly transferred my load to the dryer, added the dryer sheet, and began to dry my clothes. For several minutes, I stood ready to grab everything and head for my cell, but the switch-in order never arrived. In a few more minutes, the blood cleanup team, two specially-trained inmates who lived in D hall, arrived with their spray bottles filled with neutralizing chemicals, pails, rags, and plastic buckets. As they went about their chores, life began to return to normal, or at least what passed for normal in cell hall B West. Card games resumed, and an interrupted chess match restarted. Two groups who had been using some of the unit's exercise machines started a new round of reps, and some of the noise level quickly returned to normal.

When I got back to my cell with my clothes in about forty-five minutes, Steve Kline and Henry Jiminez were engaged in an intense conversation on the tier's rail in front of Steve's cell. Henry was espousing a line we would hear many times in the days to come. "Doug Sorenson had it coming. That lousy, fucking snitch had it coming!"

A DEGREE FOR HENRY

Steve wasn't saying much, but he did offer the thought that he hoped Sammy Dent was ready to do a lot of time in SEG.

Henry didn't agree. "It was just another fight" was his take.

Steven disagreed and made a good case. "This was a gang hit – complete with audience. I don't know how Sammy ever got into Doug's cell or onto the tier for that matter. (Rules then inside B West restricted inmates to only the tier on which they lived, and Sammy lived on the fourth tier in the front end of the building.) He doesn't even live on this section, and that itself will make for a second or third charge, depending on how upset the discipline people are when they get done with the interviews and reviewing the film. Also, Sammy did a lot of damage to a much-older guy. I think Doug's nose is broken, and did you see all that blood? No, I think Sammy is going to be in segregation for a very long time."

Steve was right: Sammy Dent got a huge sentence of 450 days. They charged him with the assault as a gang-related activity, plus being in an unauthorized area. Doug's nose was broken, and he required many stitches, which brought the number of days way up. The administration was letting all know that they were done allowing gangs to conduct their business blatantly.

In reality, little actually changed inside Stillwater; people just became a bit more careful. Even Henry Jiminez became a bit more careful in arranging his appointments and merchandise exchanges. As his school semester was going well, and he was feeling more and more like he was on the road to success, he wanted to be a bit more careful. He didn't stop doing anything, but he was more discrete. As he told his friend Steven, "I just know this is going to work out. I'm finally going to have the life I've always wanted."

Steven knew that the health course was going to be okay. He and Henry worked on that every week, almost every night. He was less sure the computer course was on track, but Henry was adamant that everything there was fine. Everything happened in the classroom, and in the computer lab, so Steven wasn't involved.

The situation in the math class was a complete mystery to Steven. Steven had no idea what was going on. From the second week of the course, Henry had declined Steven's repeated offers of assistance. His reply to any question was always "It's okay, that stuff is going pretty well. A group of us are working together, and we're getting it."

Steven didn't understand. He knew Henry didn't understand higher mathematics, but there was little that he could do.

CHARLES SLABAUGH

The next day Doug Sorenson returned to B West. He had been checked out and cleared of any charges or wrongdoing in the fight/assault. He looked terrible with two huge raccoon eyes and numerous cuts, scrapes, bruises, and of course, the broken nose. As he entered the B West front door, his smile was bright and his mood upbeat. In his mind, the entire episode proved that his theory was right. By reporting anything and everything, he put them all on notice not to mess with Doug Sorenson. And the way the prison's discipline system treated Sammy just underscored that message.

Back in Lit 1, I was trying to get Omar Oogolala's program back on track. He had never recovered from his $27 phone call and its zero results. He was very down, a real picture of depression. While he made a good show of trying to work in class, it was obvious that his mind was elsewhere, and his heart wasn't really in it anymore. Our mutual friend Dale Bishop was concerned too but thought we should just continue working and hope that time would help clear Omar's mind, so that's what we did.

Help came from a very strange situation: B West was locked down for a semiannual shakedown. During a Stillwater shakedown, the unit in question went on lockup status. Everyone sat in their cell 24/7 until every cell and every man was searched. The shakedown was announced one evening, just as everyone was re-entering the living unit after supper. Usually, we had the opportunity of returning to B West or going directly to the gym for recreation. The gym was off the main corridor, on the way back to B West. That night, when we got to the gym, two C/Os were blocking the door, saying that the gym was closed. With that news, we knew something was going on. We continued to walk to B West. Once we arrived inside B West, the PA system began, "Switch in! Switch in!" And we knew we were in for it.

A shakedown can last from three to five days. No inmates go anywhere. All work, school, medical appointments, everything, is cancelled until it is finished. Inmates sit in their cells and wait while crews of C/Os methodically go through each cell. Each man is strip-searched and then removed from his cell and handcuffed to the tier's guard rail several feet down from their cell. The idea was that the inmate cannot see what is going on in his cell while a C/O is going through everything in the cell. After what seems like an eternity, and in real time is probably less than fifteen minutes, the man is returned to his cell if the result of the search found nothing amiss. During the search, the C/O verified the serial number of all electronic property – TV, radio, electric beard trimmer, etc. – and all clothing were counted to ensure that the allowable number of each item is not exceeded. The C/O also ensures that you don't have too many books and magazines. You are allowed a total of ten. They go through your Canteen food items, and they also go through any paperwork, legal papers or other papers, and everything in your

A DEGREE FOR HENRY

cell, looking for, well, they are just looking. They also check your medications, making sure that you have only what you have been prescribed and in the proper quantities, and they check to see if you are taking them correctly.

For all the rest of the time of the shakedown, whether it's a short three-day version or a longer one, the men all sit in their cell waiting. Many sleep a great deal; much watch TV, if they own one; and some read, providing that they have things to read in their cell. Once the shakedown begins, nothing goes into or out of any cell, except meals. Inmates are prohibited from passing items between cells during a shakedown.

Meals are delivered by C/Os from the unit's regular unit staff who also deliver the mail in the afternoons. The meals are bland, meager versions of commercial TV dinners that are made in the Stillwater kitchen. They usually use two or three menus of these TV-type dinners, and hopefully, they are rotated, so no one gets the identical meal too many times in a row. Each has an entrée, one or two vegetable side dishes, a slice of bread, one half pint of 1 percent milk, and often an apple or an orange. Breakfast comes in a bag containing two individual dry cereal portions, each in its own bowl; two half pints of 1 percent milk, and sometimes an apple or an orange, and it is delivered about 3:30 AM. Those preferring their milk cold to drinking it at room temperature consume breakfast when it arrives. For everyone, a shakedown is a long tough week, but in this case, it at least allowed Doug Sorenson some time to heal up in his cell. The shakedown lasted a full five days, and Doug looked more normal when it finally ended, and the entire unit lined up to take much-needed showers.

The shakedown's end was announced the morning of the sixth day, right after breakfast was being eaten by most of the men. Most of the day was consumed with taking showers (getting 260 men through ten shower stalls takes a bit of doing), washing the accumulated dirty clothing, making phone calls, and gossiping among inmates. Some told new stories of how their unfortunate neighbor was caught with medications that he wasn't supposed to have and went immediately to the hole as a result. Some men's cell and property had been torn up, and others had hardly been bothered, or so it seemed. Actually, it was hard for many men to understand what had happened in the cell search as they had not been present during the actual search. Almost everyone had a story to share.

During the shakedown, two inmates from B West had gone to segregation. One had a drug problem, and the other had a shank, a homemade weapon, that, so the rumors said, was hidden in his overhead light fixture. He was already sending back complaints from SEG that the shank wasn't his, but that denial wouldn't

113

CHARLES SLABAUGH

matter much. The weapon was found in his cell. At Stillwater, possession was the law, all of the law.

By suppertime, I stuck my head in Steve's door to say hi. He looked pale and drawn. I asked what was wrong, and he said, "My damn stomach again. I ran out of Zantac Tuesday, and the nurse said it wasn't an emergency, so they did nothing. That woman has no idea how badly I was hurting. To make matters worse," he went on, "I hear that my student in A East went to SEG, but I don't know why. He seemed like a pretty sharp guy. I hope it isn't a big deal."

During the shakedown, the nurses from health services visit the unit daily, delivering insulin to diabetics and medications to men who normally come to health services daily (or several times a day) to receive their medications, Apparently, Steve didn't look sick to whomever he had talked to, but he sure looked a mess to me that night.

That weekend, he still felt lousy, and he was still without Zantac, but he worked hard with Henry. The coming week was midterms. The shakedown had put Henry way behind on a paper for the Health & Fitness class, and an exam was also scheduled. As he grappled with those issues, Steven asked, "How's it going with the math class?"

Henry smiled and said, "No problem. I've got it handled."

That told Steven virtually nothing, but he let the issue die. Obviously, Henry didn't want any help with math.

By Sunday afternoon, Henry's paper was about done. He would type it Monday and Tuesday afternoon in study hall. Steven didn't think Henry was ready for an exam, but Henry was confident, and he didn't want to work anymore, so they quit.

First thing Monday morning, Steven asked Jane about his new student who was missing. Jane confirmed that he was in segregation but couldn't or wouldn't say why. That was the correct answer, per DOC policy, but Steven was confused. He thought the new student, Cecil Gravenhorst, was pretty serious about earning a GED. He didn't seem like a fighter or a drug user, so Steven was confused. At the morning's break, he approached one of Gravenhorst's buddies and asked what happened.

The buddy knew the whole deal. Like many guys in prison, Gravenhorst's wife had lost interest in him, and she had filed for divorce. They had one child, a girl in her early teens. The daughter was the apple of Gravenhorst's eye, and he missed

A DEGREE FOR HENRY

her greatly. He had told his friend that the divorce was "no big deal," but his wife had now cut off his contact with his daughter, and that was gnawing at him daily. His wife no longer came to visit, and she wouldn't bring their daughter for visits either as she, the wife/mother, would have to bring the girl into the visiting room and stray for the visit, per DOC policy. To make matters worse, she had told Cecil to quit calling the girl on the phone. Unbeknownst to Cecil, she had also called the prison, told them that she didn't want Cecil calling the girl either.

The previous week Cecil had called the girl at a time when he knew his wife would be at work. He didn't know that Stillwater would enforce her wish as the custodial parent for no calls from the father, Cecil, to the daughter or herself. After his wife spoke with Cecil's case worker, Cecil's phone account was coded so that he could no longer make calls to that number. Cecil was also notified not to call his daughter by a note from the case worker.

When an inmate attempted to place any phone call, he had to use a sophisticated computer program. That program first identified the inmate and told him how much money he had in his personal phone account. When the number he dialed was answered, he could not speak to the person answering; the computer first spoke with them, telling them that the call was coming from Stillwater Prison. It also identified who was calling and told the person answering whether the call was collect or prepaid. It then required the person being called to agree to accept the call. If the right answer was forthcoming, the connection was made, and they could talk for a maximum of fifteen minutes. In the case of a blocked call, the inmate was advised that the number was blocked and the call terminated.

In this case, the computer told Cecil that the number was blocked, and it also notified his case worker that he had called the prohibited number. Within an hour, the squad's A team had Cecil in handcuffs and on his way to SEG for attempting the prohibited call. Punishment came quickly at Stillwater, as Cecil was learning.

Steven took the news calmly. He had warned Cecil not to write or call the daughter, but Cecil was determined to keep in contact with his much-loved only child. He had argued adamantly with Steven that it was his right. He and his wife were divorcing; he might be a convicted felon in prison, but Cecil was determined not to lose his only child. Now he was in segregation, and his assignment as a student in need of a GED was gone. He would now serve his SEG time, and then he would spend ninety days in the unemployed unit with no job, no income, no slot in school, and fewer privileges. Once that was over, he might get back in class and resume work on the GED, but the timing was uncertain.

CHARLES SLABAUGH

The more Steven thought about it, the angrier he became. The angrier he became, the more his stomach hurt. He was still without Zantac. He had hoped to receive a pass to see the doctor this morning, but no pass was on his door when he awoke that morning. *Maybe tomorrow*, he thought.

With the strict movement control at Stillwater, all appointments had to be scheduled the day before. The overnight watch (first watch) would print out all passes for every man in each living unit around midnight. Then as the C/Os made their hourly rounds of the tiers, they would place each man's pass on the door of his cell, affixing it under the magnetized nameplate of each man's cell door. When you awoke in the morning, each man immediately knew if he was scheduled for anything unusual that day.

By Wednesday, the week was running full speed. Lit 1 was going well; the students were glad to have the tutors back helping them with English and their numbers. Henry reported to Steve that he had finished the paper for Health & Fitness, and he said that the Health & Fitness midterm exam was "no problem." Steve Kline had even seen the doctor that morning, and a new supply of Zantac was coming from Oklahoma. Prescriptions were shipped on a next-day-delivery promise, but it might take another day or two for the Zantac to find its way to the patient. Maybe by tomorrow, he hoped, he'd get some relief from the gnawing in his gut. In general, life in B West seemed pretty much back to normal.

Even retelling of the beatdown of Dale Sorenson by Sammy Dent was pretty much old news, although Doug still bore vivid marks from his ordeal. He still moved around the unit somewhat confidently, although several members of the PMB group gave him hard looks as they passed on the flag or in the corridors. With Sammy's huge SEG sentence, no one said anything negative or even remotely threatening to Doug as he moved around the prison. The looks many others gave him were cold, hard, and unfriendly, but no one said anything. For his part, Doug always had Sammy's devastating assault very much on his mind.

Sammy had used Doug's greed for legal business to set up the beating by telling Doug that he needed help in preparing a law suit against the DOC. Although any such payments were prohibited by DOC regulations, Doug as a genuine attorney, often did such things for inmates to earn extra money. An uncle in Florida allowed Doug's customers to send the payments directly to him, where he held the money for Doug's use sometime in the future. Using that ruse, Sammy had gotten him to relax his guard and had welcomed him into his cell that fateful evening.

Chapter 10

A New Career Is Born

Early in my time in B West while working in the Education Department, I met an interesting guy in the Sunday morning Protestant chapel group, Ned Johns; an intense young black man of maybe thirty years with deep, focused eyes, a shaven head, and a lean, well-proportioned build. Softly, almost quietly spoken, he was frequently up front offering prayer or leading group singing. In the course of things, I learned that he was a student in the VT computer program, working on an AAS degree. I also came to understand that he was a lifer.

Living in a world where many denied truth and reality on a regular basis, Ned quickly caught my attention with his prayers in chapel. A frequent theme was that it didn't matter why any of us were in prison. "All have fallen short of the glory of God."

What was important was for each man to take responsibility for his own actions and for his own life and for each of us to ensure that we followed God's commandments during the rest of our lives. With that goal in mind, Ned devoted much of his free time to the seemingly-countless number of inner-city men inside Stillwater. When confronted, as he often was, but the popular inmate belief that the system was unfairly weighted against them, Ned would quietly assert that it was everyone's duty to do their best to live an honest, truthful life and, above all, to discover and follow God's will constantly in their lives.

Many times this message was not accepted, or later in the heat of the moment, it was ignored, but Ned's angry young friends soon came to understand that Ned really believed and lived the life that he was telling them about. When some of these young men asked him about the computer classes in Stillwater, Ned was

CHARLES SLABAUGH

quick to explain the pathway to those programs, and he was equally quick to offer to help them prepare for and to apply for those assignments.

Ned worked on his free time with several of these men, helping them learn the basics of numbers and English grammar; things often ignored by these men but absolutely essential for anyone hoping to conquer the GED tests. His efforts were sometimes unsuccessful with some of the men failing to master the material. More often men fell prey to the prison's uncompromising discipline system. When that happened, the young man would go to SEG, losing whatever job or program he was in.

Ned would send the men letters while they were in SEG, urging them to not lose hope and to get back on track as soon as they could. In Stillwater's system, inmates could send a kite to any staff member at no cost, but to communicate with an inmate on any subject could only be done by US Mail. Of course, many inmates would send notes in paper through an informal network of buddies, but that system wouldn't work well between living units, and it was totally ineffective in breeching the walls of the segregation unit. In those days, a no. 10 envelope cost the price of a first-class stamp, plus 8¢ at the Canteen. In a world where wages started at 25¢ an hour, that made a letter a costly luxury for most.

When their SEG time was over, if they ended up in the same unit as Ned, he quickly was back in touch, helping them through the painful ninety-day period when they were denied a job and many inmate privileges. Once that period was over, Ned continued to assist them in preparing for the exams that remained in their path.

Ned and several like-minded men even set up an informal system of helping men who lost their job or were indigent for any reason. They contributed to an informal stock of basic food and snack items, things like ramen soup packages, bags of chips, etc. When a man was down on his luck, they would drop off a few items in his cell, refusing any talk of repayment. This was in violation of DOC policy, which clearly forbade any exchange of property between offenders, but it helped many. It was a small thing but of great help to some inmates who were completely broke and feeling like no one cared.

When Ned completed his course of study in the VT computers and received his AAS degree in computer technologies, he hoped for a job as a clerk in a Minncor shop to use his new skills. As sometimes happened, there were no clerks jobs open. To avoid becoming unemployed and being subjected to the many restrictions applied to those without jobs, Ned took a job in the Recreation Department. That assignment put him in the gym or the yard all day, so Ned found himself spending

A DEGREE FOR HENRY

more time than ever with many of the same young men. He was now helping an even larger group than before.

In time, Stillwater's Transitions Department, the department charged with helping those about to be released to prepare for life outside of prison, began to use a new concept called restorative justice. A program with a nationwide following, restorative justice embraced a program of apology for bad deeds, where possible, achieving communication between those who had committed those crimes and those who had suffered from them. This was all contained in a course that was offered to all inmates. Ned quickly enrolled in the course.

To no one's surprise, Ned excelled in the course. His grades were very high, and he often took the lead in classroom discussions, giving the somewhat bland text life and believability. At the conclusion of the course, the three staff members working with the group (the education director Ms. Polinski, the transitions manager, and a literacy teacher) asked Ned what he thought of the course. His reply was positive and direct: He loved the idea of the course but felt that the text, as written, was a bit off the mark and really wasn't connecting with the Stillwater audience. Asked to go on, Ned suggested that some of the material might play well in a well-to-do, mostly-white suburb, but that it struck inner-city men as phony or at best unrealistic.

Smiling, Ms. Polinski asked, "Would you like to help us fix it?"

Without hesitation, Ned said, "Absolutely."

Within days, he was no longer in a recreation assignment but had been hired as transitions tutor. In about eight weeks, the group, with Ned doing most of the heavy lifting, had rewritten the curriculum. Then Ms. Polinski asked Ned the big question: "Now would you like to become the primary teacher for the course?"

Again, without hesitation, Ned said, "Absolutely!"

He was off and running to a new career as a teacher. The result was an absolute win for everyone. Those enrolled in the class were given a more realistic course of study, with a motivated teacher they could easily relate to, and the DOC saw many more students emerging from the program better prepared for life outside of prison.

Even in a world as dark, bureaucratic, and heavily structured as Stillwater Prison, sometimes the right man got the job!

Chapter 11

NOT EVERYONE FITS THE MOLD

As I became more familiar with the routine of the 260 men who lived in B West, most seemed to fit into one of several groups: Some men were workout fanatics – always using B West's several exercise and fitness machines that dotted the flag and always being at the front of the line moving from the gym or the yard. These men never seemed to be able to work their muscles often enough or hard enough. As a group, they were in excellent physical shape. Others were always at the flag's eight six-man card and game tables. Some played cards and often specialized in one game or in just one version of a game. Some played chess, and a few of them became quite good at it.

Many of the Hispanics hung out together. Usually, this group was divided by nationality, with Mexicans hanging out only with other Mexicans, Cubans only with Cubans, and so on. Among the Mexicans and the Puerto Ricans, there were frequently subdivisions based on gang affiliations, with those gang loyalties becoming more distinct than was the basic nationality distinction. Like the Hispanics, the blacks seemed to stick together, again with gang affiliations often becoming more important to many members of the group.

The Asians were interesting. As a young man in the US Army, I had served in Vietnam, and I well remembered how each of Southeast Asia's nationalities seemed to dislike, often intensely, all members of other Southeast Asian nationalities. Vietnamese disliked Laos, and Thais didn't like Hmongs. As I remember it from 1969 and 1970, none of them liked the Cambodians, or at least that was my experience. It was different inside Stillwater. All the Asians hung out together, eating together, hanging out together, and even defending one another from all others.

A DEGREE FOR HENRY

Those in the Aryan white power groups were very close and tight. Their bond seemed strong and solid, and they were very cohesive. To anyone foolish enough to challenge them, they were most formidable.

Equally formidable to any challenge, the Natives were a tight group. They sought to do everything, whenever possible, as a group, living and working only with other Natives. The Natives were constantly thwarted in their desire to all work the same job, but the DOC's absolute policy was that all living areas and work areas have an ethnic makeup that represented the population of the entire prison. When too many Natives showed up on a specific job's population, new Native applicants would not be accepted. In some cases, Natives were arbitrarily transferred to different assignments just to maintain a balance of the job's makeup, which was precisely the opposite of the intention of the Natives, but it fulfilled the DOC's policy.

They had even managed to secure DOC endorsement of the right to worship as a group and in an area set aside for their exclusive use. When other groups worshiped in the chapel (actually designated as the religious services area – a gift many years before to the prison from the Roman Catholic Diocese of St. Paul and Minneapolis), the Natives worshiped together in a structure resembling a traditional teepee located away from everything else, outside of the regular living area.

Wherever you looked inside Stillwater, you saw evidence of gangs. Men spent their time only with members of their gang. They sought to work only with gang members, they spent their free time with gang members, and they were quick to defend members of their gang from any and all threats, real or perceived. The DOC was equally quick and determined to resist anything they determined to be evidence of gang influence or membership. The nicer athletic sneakers we ordered from the JCPenny catalog and later purchased from the DOC-run Minncor Canteen could only be purchased in specific, non-gang colors. An inmate flashing what was known or thought to be a gang sign was subject to immediate and decisive discipline.

To the DOC, gangs represented a real and serious threat. Gangs helped foster the drug culture and were frequently the cause of violent acts inside the prison. With that knowledge, the DOC's assault on anything and everything resembling any gang activity was unrelenting.

To young gang members, the gang represented home, security, and a comfort zone. On the outside, gangs controlled the social and economic life they had grown up in. Just about everyone they knew belonged to the gang. To them, it was

CHARLES SLABAUGH

unthinkable not to belong. They were not only willing to belong, but they also wanted to belong, and many had gone through a great deal to become a member. To be told in prison that the gang was a bad thing was just another example of "the man" just not getting it.

To a young inmate, fresh off the bus from MCF - St. Cloud, encountering a huge, long block of identical cold cells and several hundred indifferent or threatening new faces; to find someone or a group of young people who recognized and accepted him as an equal or as a brother was a very welcoming thing. For these young men, their gang membership, or the promise of membership to come, was of great comfort and help as they navigated the dark and often treacherous waters of prison life.

Being a gang member gave them immediate acceptance, identity, and friendship. If they were without means to acquire good shoes, sweats, or even extra food, the gang would often fill that need. True, this support often came at a price to be paid later, but to belong to the gang was a huge positive deal to these young men, and they embraced membership enthusiastically, immediately, and gratefully. They belonged.

There were to be sure a few loners inside the inmate community, but they were in the minority. One who caught my eye early on was Owen Tofte, a middle-aged, slightly-built fellow with a quiet manner. Owen was one of the many B West unit swampers. He was one of the inmates charged with keeping B West clean and livable.

Most swampers sought to minimize the time they spent on the actual job, and in fact, most had little to do. For example, each tier had a swamper assigned. First thing in the morning, most would sweep and then wet mop the tier, a distance of may be 400 x 3 feet. This area called the catwalk was the walkway in front of the cells. Individual inmates were responsible for cleaning inside their individual cells. The more industrious swamper might then dust the long guard rail, but in less than an hour, they were done and would return to bed, the card/game tables, or to the workout equipment. If something would soil their area, like a mug of coffee being spilled, they might clean that up, but in most cases, their daily routine was a short quick one.

Owen was an exception. He cleaned the unit's large gang-type showers in the back of the living unit. B West had ten shower heads that wrapped around the north end of the unit. Each was ceramic-tiled on the floor and in the back, with a waist-high wall in front, which was also tiled in ceramic. The shower area's floor

A DEGREE FOR HENRY

was covered with heavy black rubberized mats, and the swamper was supposed to keep the entire area clean. No easy task with 260 men using the showers daily.

Owen did his job thoroughly and well, always removing the rubberized mats from the entire shower area and then vigorously scrubbing the tile. He kept everything as clean and sanitary as possible, keeping the ever-present danger of athlete's foot infection under control. He cleaned the showers in the morning, after most of us had gone to work, so I didn't initially meet him in the unit. We met at the Sunday Protestant Christian service, where he was a regular participant.

One Sunday we ended up in the same row and shared a hymnal. After the service, we chatted in the religious service center's lobby while we waited to be released back to our living unit. Responding to my question as to his hometown, he told me that he worked as a carpenter in a small town in the central part of the state. He went on to explain that he and his wife had been sent to prison for sexual crimes against their children: two sons and a daughter.

His admission of guilt, especially for such a crime, amazed me. While the general category of sexual crimes represented the largest category for the Minnesota Department of Corrections, few inmates were at all forthcoming in admitting such things. Sexual offenders (SOs as they were called by many) were in an extremely-dangerous position inside the prison, especially those whose cases involved children. Held in contempt by many, they were actually under the very real threat of physical harm from some. It was not at all unusual for an SO to be assaulted for no apparent reason by others. As a result, most men with an SO case were reluctant to admit that fact casually. Yet here was this quiet, serious fellow, openly telling me about it.

He said it all began as a game between him and his wife. Gradually, they brought all three children into the game until it became a family activity. This went on for quite some time, several years.

During a routine doctor's visit for the daughter, the illicit play came to light. When the authorities were made aware of what was going on, both parents were arrested and ultimately imprisoned for long terms. The children were made wards of the court. Ultimately, they were placed with an aunt and uncle, and Owen and his wife had their parental rights terminated. Soon after arriving at MCF – Stillwater, Owen was served with legal papers again. His wife was divorcing him.

He told me the entire story over a cup of coffee, never qualifying anything, and ending the tale by saying that the blame was entirely his. He said he and his wife had enjoyed the game but that he should have never allowed it to begin, and that he should have stopped it long before the doctor intervened.

While in county jail for over a year, awaiting the disposition of the case, some Christian evangelists had brought the word of God to Owen. Without hesitation or qualification, he said he knew what an awful sin he had committed. He quickly became an articulate and tireless Christian preacher in jail and in prison. He said that he really was uncomfortable speaking to groups, although he had done so. He preferred to speak one-to-one with people as he was with me.

Unlike most unit swampers, who hurried through their duties in early in the morning so they could then get on with what they preferred to do, Owen spent every morning meticulously cleaning B West's showers. He removed all the large heavy rubberized mats from each area of the shower and painstakingly scrubbed all the ceramic surfaces daily, with Sunday being the only exception. Sunday was his day off.

By late in the morning, the entire shower area was literally sparkling; it was so clean. Then Owen would begin his rounds. With a paperbound Bible in hand, he would visit all of B West's unemployed inmates who were locked in all day, except for meals; most of them jammed in two to a six-by-nine cell.

If the inmate was awake, Owen would greet him and ask how the day was going. If the man or men were asleep, he would not disturb them, but he would try again after lunch and the noon count. When he found men awake, he would offer to share the word of God with them. If the inmate or inmates declined, Owen would smile and ask if they needed anything. Ice was a frequent request, and Owen would take their container through the bars and then visit one of B West's two large ice machines on the flag, returning with the requested ice. If they needed toilet paper or some other supply item that he could access, he would bring that item to them.

Initially, when he began this routine, and occasionally later with a new man in the unit, Owen's request to share the word was met with hostility. When that happened, he would quietly smile and say, "Not a problem," and then ask about any other non-spiritual needs. Very quickly, the word spread that this was indeed a good guy who just wanted to help. In this way, Owen passed his days in B West.

In time, I came to know him pretty well, and we talked often. Owen had no doubt that he had sinned greatly, but he was equally certain of God's forgiveness and of his need to love and serve these men. After four years on the job, when the Department of Correction's policy mandated a move to a new job assignment, he asked for a similar assignment in a different unit, and he was moved to A East,

A DEGREE FOR HENRY

which then housed the Education Department's students. In short order, A East had the cleanest showers inside Stillwater, and A East's unemployed, locked-in men began to have a helpful visitor to their locked cell doors.

Owen never forced his Christian beliefs on anyone. While he certainly encountered men with no interest in finding their salvation is Christ, he found others with sincerely-held beliefs in other religions; Islam, Moorish Science, Wiccan, and various other non-Christian beliefs were all represented in Stillwater's population. Owen did find many yearning to learn, understand, and to find peace. Most of these men had grown up with Christian parents or caregivers but had allowed the course of their life to take them away from that path.

As a swamper, Owen was allowed access to all the tiers of B West. Occasionally, a new C/O in the unit would ask what he was doing or why he was on a specific tier or in a certain area. Once they understood what he was doing and the way he was doing it, his visits went on unencumbered. The B West unemployed men came to look forward to Owen's visits, and most C/Os came to appreciate his calming influence on men with little to look forward to in their daily routine.

One day I observed Owen having a special order purchase voucher signed by the C/O at the main desk. These vouchers were used when we were ordering something from an outside vendor. We submitted them to the Property Department, signed by a C/O, with an addressed envelope attached addressed to the vendor. I first assumed that Owen was ordering some of the casual clothing almost all of us wore when we were not working our job assignment. We could order gray T-shirts, sweatpants, shorts, and athletic shirts from Minncor Industries, and we could order books and other approved materials from outside approved vendors. We could also order certain models of better athletic sneakers from the JCPenny catalog. The clothing was more comfortable than the regular state-issue, and this was somewhat of a status item with some of the men, distinguishing those with money from those without.

Being a bit nosy, I asked Owen what he was ordering. Lowering his voice, Owen told me that he was sending money out to his children. Owen went on to explain that he sent money out every month for his kids. He and his wife had done awful things to the children, he went on, and while he doubted that he would ever be allowed to see his children again, he sent the small amount of money to them every month. His uncle and aunt who were raising the children were very good to them. Owen was sure they wanted for nothing, but he sent what money he could anyway. At that point, he had never heard anything from either the aunt or uncle or the kids, but that didn't seem to bother him.

CHARLES SLABAUGH

Under the regulations, the children were wards of the court, as Owen and his wife's parental rights had been terminated, and he was denied any contact with them, so he sent the money to the county's welfare office, hoping it would reach the kids. Trying to explain my nosy question, I said that I was hoping that maybe he was doing something for himself – some comfortable sweats or maybe even a nice Bible, as I had always noticed that he carried a much-worn paperbound Bible, which I was sure he had picked up in the chapel. With a smile, Owen assured me that "the Lord provides all that I need. I have plenty of clothes, and the paperbound Bibles are brimming with God's word and peace. I need nothing else."

In a world filled with unrest, self-centeredness, and unhappiness, Owen was a rock of calm and well-ordered priorities.

Chapter 12

Bad Decision

Like many men in prison, Cecil Gravenhorst never thought he would end up inside any prison. Growing up on the famed Minnesota Iron Range, he loved the outdoors. Starting when he was young, he hunted, fished, trapped, or just walked in the forest at every opportunity. Never much for books, he quit high school in the eleventh grade, joining his father and elder brother in the mines of the Iron Range.

Within a year, he and his sweetheart Sara married, and the next year their daughter Geri was born. Cecil and Sara bought an older mobile home and placed it in the forest outside of town, on a lot owned by Cecil's dad. The mobile home was older and primitive, with no working bath or shower, but they both loved living in the woods. Every day or two they would go to the home of Cecil's parents to shower and clean up. They also did their laundry at the home of Cecil's parents. For several years, things went well. Cecil continued to hunt every weekend and most afternoons after work. The Iron Range was full of wild game. From deer to moose to even bears, Cecil harvested them all, often providing meat not only for their table, but often for his parents' and his brother's homes too.

As Geri grew, she became her dad's best buddy. Often going into the woods with him, she learned to move quietly, and at a very early age, she learned to shoot. Cecil's many rifles and shotguns were too large for her small frame, so at the age of eight, he bought her a single-shot pistol. She grew to love going out with Cecil, and their bond grew very strong.

As the years passed, Sara worked in the mining company's office. She began to wish for a more modern house with a working bathroom, hot water, and things like her friends at work enjoyed. Cecil agreed but pointed out that there was no

CHARLES SLABAUGH

money for such things. They were earning good money and the work was steady, but whenever they got a little money ahead, Cecil would purchase another gun, an ATV, or a bigger boat. To Sara, the growing collection of Cecil's hunting stuff was a growing rival and proof to her that Cecil didn't really care what she wanted or thought.

Cecil's mother understood her son, and she also understood her daughter-in-law's desire for a nicer home. When Sara went back to work, Cecil's mother, who was home all day, offered to take Geri so they could avoid the expense of child care. Sara was delighted, thinking that would make the family's savings grow more quickly. To Cecil, this meant that he could continue to add to his growing gun collection at a faster clip.

Sara grew more and more unhappy, while Cecil seemed mostly not to notice. Every day he rushed to his parents' home after work to pick up Geri, so they would head for the woods. To Cecil, life was grand and fun. To Sara, life was a growing ordeal. Cecil and Sara began to argue and fight about little things. Before long, Sara announced that she was going to leave unless things changed and changed quickly. Cecil's answer was "Go anywhere you want, but Geri stays with me. We've got it good. You just don't understand how good our life really is."

Two days later, Cecil arrived at his parents' home for Geri. Cecil's mother was confused. That morning Sara had come by with Geri, as usual, but had not left her. Sara said Geri had a doctor's appointment and wouldn't be staying that day. Cecil had known nothing about any doctor's appointment. He drove home confused.

The house was empty when he got there, with a note on the table. In the note, Sara said that she was leaving. She said she didn't want to live that way any longer. She was taking Geri, and she wanted a divorce. Cecil was beside himself: He couldn't understand what had made Sara so unhappy. He returned to his parents' home and told them what was going on with his family.

His mother didn't say much. She had known for some time that Sara wanted a nicer home, but she had kept quiet. Cecil's dad was surprised and angry, like Cecil. "What does that girl have in her head?" he roared. "She's got a good house and a good man. She wants too much!"

The next morning Cecil went to work as usual. After the midmorning break, he went to the office where Sara worked. His intention was to find out where Geri was. When he walked into the office where Sara worked, her desk was empty. He saw her boss and asked where Sara was. Her boss said that Sara had called in

A DEGREE FOR HENRY

sick the day before. Cecil was now more concerned, confused, and angry as he left the office.

Thinking it over, he headed back to the mine's entrance. He decided that Sara must have gone to her sister's home which was 15 miles away. Without telling anyone where he was going or even punching out on the time clock, Cecil got in his truck and headed for the home of Sara's sister. As he drove there, he grew more and more angry. To Cecil, Sara could leave if she wished, but there was no way she could have Geri. He and Geri belonged together. How did Sara think that she could do this?

When he arrived at the home of Maud, Sara's sister, Cecil parked and banged on the door. In a moment, Maud's live-in boyfriend, an older man named Steve, opened the door. He knew Cecil and began to say, "Hell-o."

Cecil spoke at the same time. "Where are Sara and my Geri?"

Steve dropped his eyes and with the screen door still shut, said, "I can't tell you."

With that, Steve closed the main door.

Cecil couldn't believe it. Steve was a part of this; he was helping Sara steal Geri. Cecil jerked the screen door open and tried the main door. Steve had gotten it locked. In a rage, Cecil kicked it once, twice; then putting all his might behind it, Cecil forced it open as the frame splintered. With splinters flying everywhere, Cecil was inside.

Steve had moved to a bookcase. From an open door, his hand came out with a revolver. Cecil couldn't believe it; Steve was now pointing that gun directly at him.

"Stop right where you are, Cecil, or I'll shoot you just as sure as hell!" Steve shouted. "Sara doesn't want to see you. If you're smart, you'll get the hell out of here right now. I'm dead serious, Cecil, get the hell out of here . . . Now!"

Cecil stopped moving and began to cry. "All I want is my daughter. If Sara is leaving, that's okay, I guess, but I want my daughter."

"Geri's with her mom, where she belongs. If you're smart, you'll leave it at that. Cecil, I've been through a divorce. Believe me, no court in the world's going to take a little girl away from her mother, especially a mother like Sara, and give her to you."

CHARLES SLABAUGH

With that, Cecil began to cry again. Without thinking, Steve walked toward him, at the same time saying, "I know it's tough. Be smart, get a good lawyer, and let him work out a fair visitation schedule for you."

When Cecil heard visitation, his arm slapped at the gun in Steve's hand. With his other hand, he shoved Steve backward into a low coffee table. As Steve fell, the gun hit the floor. Cecil ran over, picked it up, and aimed it at Steve. Steve was getting up, holding his head, which had hit the edge of a standing ashtray. He was bleeding, and he was angry. Taking a step toward Cecil, he shouted, "Look, you son of a bitch, if you want trouble . . ."

That's as far as he got, Cecil shot him right in the face. The gun, a Smith & Wesson .357 Magnum, roared, and the bullet entered Steve's upper lip, just below the nose. It made a small entry hole, but the force of the blast blew the back out of Steve's head.

Cecil looked at the wreckage of Steve's head. *This was bad*, he thought. *Now I've got to run but not without Geri.* In an instant, he thought, *Where's Maud?*

The answer came immediately: On a weekday morning like this, Maud would be at work. She had a job in a small town in the neighboring county about twenty minutes away.

Shoving the revolver in his pocket, Cecil went out to his pickup. Maud and Steve's house was out in the county, with no close neighbors. Everything seemed normal; no one had heard the shot.

Cecil drove west to Maud's work. Arriving at the building that housed the business she worked for, Cecil went inside and asked the receptionist for Maud. When Maud came out of the back, the smile on her face vanished when she saw Cecil.

"What are you doing here?" came out of her mouth.

"I need to talk with you, Maud. I can't find Sara or Geri, and I'm worried about them," Cecil began.

"They're all right, but, Cecil, they don't want to see you."

Cecil moaned, "What do you mean Geri doesn't want to see me? She's my daughter, and I love her."

A DEGREE FOR HENRY

"She loves you too, I know that," Maud said, "but she's a little girl, and she's better off with her mother. You need to respect this, Cecil."

Cecil began to cry, then he caught himself. "Maud, please come out and talk with me for a minute. I really need your help, please!" he begged.

The others in the small office were pretending not to listen to them, but Maud knew that wasn't true. This was a small business in a small town. Everyone listened to everyone's business. With that in mind, Maud said, "Okay, but just for a minute."

Cecil followed her outside and motioned to his pickup. Once they were both inside the cab, Cecil's voice dropped, and he said, "Okay, where are they?"

"I can't tell you," Maud began. "Sara said you'd be upset. She doesn't want to hurt or anger you, but she's unhappy. She's tired of that old trailer without even a shower. She wants to live better than that."

"Oh, she wants a fucking shower. She can have anything she wants, but she can't have Geri. That little girl is my whole life!"

Maud grimaced, "Cecil, you're not being realistic. You can't take care of a young girl, you can hardly take care of yourself. You need to be realistic."

At that point, Cecil snapped and pulled the revolver out of his jacket's pocket. "Maud, I've always liked you. You were always okay to me, but if you don't tell me where Geri is, I'm going to kill you, just like I killed Steve."

"Steve! You killed Steve! Are you nuts? Sara and Geri are gone, and you will never find them!"

The sound of the gun filled every corner of the pickup's small cab. The bullet tore through Maud's middle and went right through the truck's door panel too as it smashed the life out of Maud.

As the sound's echo died down, the door to the small office burst open as the people from inside ran out to see what had just happened. Cecil dropped the gun on the seat next to Maud's lifeless form, turned on the ignition key, and headed down Highway 169 South, toward Grand Rapids. For a few minutes, Cecil was thinking, *Where could she be? I've got to find Geri, and we'll run for the woods.*

CHARLES SLABAUGH

He had less than $17 in his jeans, but he hadn't gotten that far in his planning yet. Suddenly, a flashing red light filled his rearview mirror, and two police cars were pulling across his path, 200 yards ahead. It really wasn't much of car chase, and it was over.

Cecil spent over a year in county jail. The family stood by him, but he was represented by a public defender. Later, at Stillwater, Cecil would learn how the inmates called them public pretenders, but at that point, all Cecil knew was that his lawyer was a good one. Cecil's case was complicated as his two victims were killed in different counties, and both counties wanted their pound of retribution for the "wanton murder of two fine citizens." Cecil had not known it, but Steve was a former corrections officer, so many of the deputies in the small county jail where he was held in were very unfriendly, accusing Cecil of "killing my brother officer."

In the end, his attorney convinced Cecil and his family to take a plea to first-degree murder in each county. Cecil's attorney mounted no defense. He didn't even attempt to combine the two trials into one, convincing Cecil to plead guilty, accepting the most extreme sentence possible under Minnesota law. The afternoon of his sentencing Cecil arrived inside Stillwater Prison with two back-to-back "life without parole" sentences and a very sour attitude. Complicating his situation, Cecil had not graduated from high school. Lacking a diploma, DOC policy mandated that he go to school to earn his GED diploma rather than allowing him to take a regular job.

Cecil had never been a strong student. Now he had no choice but to try to learn and get his diploma. At first, he went to class for half of the day and just hung out for the rest of the day in his cell. As a half-time student, his prison pay amounted to almost nothing, but his family sent money every month. They also made the long drive from the Iron Range to Bayport every month for a three-hour extended visit. The DOC allowed visitors traveling more than 100 miles one way to visit for the extra hour. Inmates were allowed two such extended visits each month. Cecil's dad even proposed that he and Cecil's mother move to Bayport so they could visit several times a week, but they both had good jobs on the Iron Range, so they couldn't do that. Cecil's mom had started working after the trouble started just to fill her days.

Cecil was almost immediately assigned to the literacy program. Because of his low reading and math scores, he joined Lit 1. For several months, he made little progress in class, but he learned the ropes of life inside Stillwater, and he got comfortable with life in A East. He became a regular at the gym, using the various weight-training machines, and he made some friends.

A DEGREE FOR HENRY

Just as he was getting accustomed to being in school, Cecil tried to call his daughter, against the wishes of his wife. As a result of making an unauthorized call, Cecil lost his assignment, went to SEG, and then sat unemployed for over ninety days.

Finally, he was rehired as a student, and he then got back to the business of earning his GED diploma. Cecil was assigned to several tutors, but nothing seemed to fit. He was attending school but accomplishing little.

After a few months, a new tutor joined Lit 1. Harold Sullivan was new in Stillwater, serving a long sentence for murder. Harold was smart, with good people skills and high reading and math scores, so Jane Halverson quickly recruited him as a tutor. With twenty-two tutors in her program, someone was always being transferred to a different prison, going to segregation on a violation, or just moving on to a different job; so Jane always had room for a promising prospect.

Using Harold's arrival as an excuse, Jane rearranged several of the tutor-student pairings in the class that morning, and Harold ended up with Cecil as a morning student. As she introduced the two, Jane got right to the point with Cecil. "Cecil, Harold can really help you, if you are willing to roll up your sleeves and get to work. I know that you are not happy to be in school, but you have little choice here. You must earn your GED before you can get any other job, and that isn't going to happen until you raise your reading and math scores. Once you get your GED, you have many options, but today that is your only choice."

Cecil didn't like being the focus of Jane's attention, and he meekly said, "I've never done well in school. When I was a kid, I was always in special ed."

He hoped that would blunt Jane's attack, but it didn't.

"I know that, Cecil, but I also believe that you can do this. It won't be easy, and it may not happen quickly, but you can make this happen. I'll tell you what, Cecil, when you earn your GED diploma, I'll hire you as a tutor right here in Lit 1. What would your family think of that?"

With that, Jane returned to her desk.

Harold and Cecil finished the period working in a basic reading book. Harold quickly understood that his new student really couldn't read well, but he was friendly enough and seemed fairly bright. When the morning period ended, Cecil went to lunch and then stopped in the gym, working up a sweat on several machines.

That night Harold thought a bit about Cecil. In an unusual move, Jane had given Harold three students. Cecil was just part of his focus. One of the students, Soma Eckonalanza, a refugee from East Africa was leaving soon, but the third student, Omar Oogolala, was also a GED hopeful very much in need of raising his reading score. Harold really wanted to motivate Cecil.

That night, on his bunk, Cecil thought about what Jane had said. Could he really become a tutor, he mused. All his life, Cecil had never really thought that he was good at anything, except hunting, fishing, and being in the woods. *Could I really do it?* Cecil wondered as sleep overtook him.

The next morning Harold got right down to business, asking Cecil what he had been doing with his life. Cecil's answers were vague, indicating that he had done lots of things with no plan or overall direction. Harold said, "It's really pretty simple. We've got to improve your reading level. The GED tests require a higher reading level than you have. We can tackle that successfully if you are ready to work extra hard. What do you say, Cecil? How important is this to you?"

All his life, no one had ever asked Cecil if he was willing to work hard. Without hesitation, Cecil said, "Sure, I'll work. Do you really think that I can do this? I've never been very good in school. I was always in special ed. My folks said it was okay. I guess I'm just dumb."

Harold smiled. "Well, I don't think you're dumb. Some of us learn differently from others. We just need to find what approach works best for you. What do you like to do?"

Cecil's answer was quick. "My daughter and I used to go to the woods to hunt, trap, and fish. It was great."

Later that morning, when the class had a chance to visit the library, Harold said to his three students, "Come on, guys. Let's see what we can find interesting in the library today."

In Harold's mind, the key to reading was to find something that the men were interested in. For Cecil, they found Jack London's epic *White Fang* and a newer book on elk hunting.

In the next few weeks, Harold continued to find things for Cecil to read that interested him. Slowly, almost without noticing it, Cecil's reading began to improve. As he finished a book, he and Harold would discuss it, and often Harold encouraged Cecil to write a report on the book.

A DEGREE FOR HENRY

Harold had Cecil begin to prepare for one of the GED tests, the reading test, which Harold thought was the easiest of the five tests. As Harold explained it to Cecil, "We will do these one at a time. It's easier that way."

That weekend Cecil's family came for a visit on Saturday. For several months, Cecil was finding it harder and harder to say goodbye to them when visits ended. He knew it was silly, but seeing them leave was causing him much pain and trauma. After they left, he wrote a kite to the visiting room and removed their names from his list of approved visitors. He then wrote them a letter, explaining that he just couldn't bear to see them leave. He also told them that it was too painful to speak with them on the phone. As a result, he would no longer be calling them. He said, "I'm going to be here forever, I guess, and I've got to do this alone."

His father was angry, not understanding his son's decision. His mother was very upset, but she understood his pain and his decision.

One day Cecil was thinking about a story he had just read, and he commented, "He was just like me, a fat kid."

Harold stopped him and said, "Why do you say that? You're not fat."

Cecil replied, "Yes, I am. I've always been heavy, but since I've come to prison, I've gained even more weight. I'm fat."

Harold said then, "If you want to lose some weight and get into better shape, you can do that. When you go over to the library tomorrow, let's look for a book on nutrition. You can lick this issue too."

The next day Cecil did just that; he checked out a book on eating right and another on physical fitness. As he read those books and others, Cecil learned about food, how some of it helps us grow lean and strong and how some of it, like the chips and cakes he ate so many of, just added pounds. It was hard finding good things to eat from the prison's centralized Minncor Canteen. The Canteen's catalog was loaded with things young men loved to eat, but Cecil was learning that there were better choices. Cecil began to improve and reduce his overall food intake. He learned that, like many in prison, he often ate when he was bored or was feeling low. To his surprise, he realized that when he was feeling unhappy about being in prison for the rest of his life, a bag of chips or a package of cupcakes made him feel better.

As part of his new reading program, Cecil was reading about physical fitness, and he became interested in getting stronger too. With Harold's encouragement, he started doing laps on Stillwater's track around the main yard; first by just

CHARLES SLABAUGH

walking and then by running. It didn't come easily or quickly, but by the end of the year; Cecil was running almost every day than the main yard was open. In the time when he was locked in his six-by-nine cell, which was often at Stillwater, Cecil began working out in his cell. It took him by surprise at year end when Jane mentioned that he looked thinner. Using the gym's scale, he saw that he was down from his former weight of 260 pounds to 241 pounds. Delighted, he redoubled his running and resolved to cut out chips and cakes completely.

By July 4, Cecil was less than 210 pounds, and to everyone's delight, he had passed two of the five GED tests: reading and science. Cecil was more amazed than anyone; he had never dreamed that he could change his life so dramatically.

The greatest pain in his life was his total separation from Geri. Since that awful day, he had absolutely no contact with Sara, and he had heard nothing from Geri who was now eleven years old. Early in his time at Stillwater, he had tried to phone Geri after being told not to do so by his case worker. That had resulted in an immediate trip to SEG, his being removed from Lit class, and then spending over one hundred days unemployed until Jane rehired him as a student. "When she is eighteen, she will come to see me," Cecil told himself. "This is just her mother's influence because of what I did to Maud and Steve."

By the end of that year, Cecil had passed four of the GED exams, only the math test had eluded him. Some of the test's content were not a problem for Cecil, but the exam went into algebra, and algebra was very hard for Cecil. He finally conquered that test too.

That July Cecil attended graduation in Stillwater's visiting room. Through the entire ceremony, he wished his mother could have come, but his earlier decision to remove her from his visiting list made her attendance impossible. He wondered what his mom would have said if she had seen him that day. He was graduating, and he was down to 170 pounds. On his 6-foot-2-inch frame, he was a very slender fit young man. True to her word, Jane had immediately hired him as a tutor. He knew his mom would have loved to know that he wondered how his parents were doing. Most of all, he wondered what Geri was doing.

Chapter 13

THE SOUND OF MUSIC

As soon as I arrived at Stillwater, I began attending Christian religious services in the chapel. Initially, I went to Sunday Protestant services, which were held in the midmorning after breakfast. After a few years, I tried the Roman Catholic service, which were held very early in the morning on Sunday at 6:40 AM. I found that the Roman Catholic service was very much like the traditional High Church Episcopal services that I had grown up with. Ultimately, I became a regular Catholic worshiper.

I soon noticed that the services were quite different, with large groups attending the Protestant services, which were conducted by a rotation of outside volunteer groups representing the many versions of Protestantism. Protestant services usually filled the room's seventy seats. The Catholic mass was a shorter affair attended by about half as many inmates. That service was conducted by Stillwater's staff chaplain, director of religious services), an older Catholic priest, Fr. Sean Gilbertson. The services had one thing in common: a middle-aged inmate of solid build named Ben Simonton. If you attended just about any Christian service at Stillwater, you quickly noticed Ben because of his beautiful tenor voice. Ben joined in all the singing at the Protestant services, and he often sang a solo at some point in the service. The Catholics were not as much into music, but Ben always sang a solo during communion. Most of us were poor singers, but Ben was good, very good.

Ben worked closely with Father Gilbertson, preparing for his Sunday communion solo. The chaplain would sometimes obtain instrumental records on the CD format for Ben to use in his solo, and he would also arrange for Ben to visit the chapel during the week on a pass to practice with the recording. During my

CHARLES SLABAUGH

first year at Stillwater, Ben missed a Sunday performance, which we all noticed immediately. When you sang as poorly as most of us, losing an accomplished vocalist was quickly noticed. We soon heard that Ben was in the hole. A few weeks later, I was doing my laundry in the back half of B West, and I saw Ben locked in a cell on the flag. I walked over, extending my sympathies for his dilemma and asking if he needed ice, toilet paper, or anything else. Ben quickly declined but thanked me for the offer. "I'm fine," he began. "I've got everything that I need. This is all my own fault anyway. I forgot and left one of Father's CDs in my pocket when I left the chapel. It's plastic, so it went right through the metal detector, but when I returned to A East, they decided to do a random pat-down, and they found it. I was really lucky, they could have charged me with having a weapon, but they didn't."

As I was folding my clothes, I considered what Ben had shared with me. For a simple, innocent mistake, he had (1) gone to SEG for eight days, (2) lost his job as a clerk in Minncor, (3) would now spend ninety days as a UI with few privileges and no income locked in his cell 23/7. After all that, he was telling me how fortunate he was.

About a year later, Ben was long since back at his clerk's job, although he had to start over at the bottom of the prison wage scale, and he was again singing every Sunday in the chapel. The prison grapevine spreads the news that he was sick: Cancer was the word. Like most prison news, the word spread quickly among Ben's friends and admirers, but there were several versions of the story going around. One version had him very sick with only a few weeks to live. Another version had him afflicted with a relatively-minor version of the scourge, it was no big deal. This was typical of prison rumors; they seldom had the story either complete or correct, and often one version of a rumor was in complete conflict with another version. I resolved to get to the truth.

The next Sunday morning I entered the chapel for the 6:40 mass. After checking in with the C/O on duty and giving him my ID and my chapel pass, I looked for Ben. I quickly found him in the chapel's storage room, loading the CD of music for the day into a portable boom box we used for services. After a quick "Hell-o, how are you doing?" I got right to the matter. "Ben," I began, "I hear you've got health troubles. I hope it's nothing serious."

Ben smiled and said, "Well, I wish it weren't serious, but cancer is never good news. I've got cancer in my prostate and colon. The doctor wants to have more tests done, but he thinks it's manageable."

A DEGREE FOR HENRY

After a moment, Father Gilbertson came into the room, saying, "Are we ready, Ben?"

Ben nodded yes, and I headed into the main room for mass.

As we left the chapel forty-five minutes later, I had only a brief moment to wish Ben the best before we were all released to return to our living units.

Modern American prisons have good up-to-date medical systems, complete with good equipment, doctors, dentists, and skilled nursing staffs. At Stillwater, we no longer had a hospital-type unit. Men needing extreme care were transferred to a St. Paul area hospital, and convalescent services were provided inside the nearby supermax prison, Oak Park Heights. Despite all those positive things, I had already learned that prison – any prison – isn't a great place to be sick. Security concerns are always the first priority, and at Stillwater, inmates were locked in their cells for many hours of every day. All these considerations could and often did lead to delays in responding to situations in which an inmate with the medical or issue was hoping for quick action.

As the weeks passed after the news of Ben's problems had been announced, I didn't see him very often, and when I did see him and was able to ask how things were going, he always had the same answer: "I'm still waiting. Nothing has happened."

I could tell that he was very concerned about the situation, but he never had much to say, other than to confirm that he was still waiting.

After well over another month of nothing happening, one Sunday, as the weekly mass was ending, Father Gilbertson said, "Ben Simonton has an announcement for us."

With that, Ben stood up and said, "Several of you have been asking about my medical problems and have been wondering when I'm going to begin treatment. The plan was that I would be sent to Oak Park or directly to a hospital for more tests and to let a specialist make a confirming diagnosis. I've been waiting for weeks – actually, two months – but so far, nothing has happened. You know how it is in here, they treat all transfers or moves to another facility as though they were national security issues, and so far, nothing has happened. I know nothing. I've thought this over and considered everything prayerfully. I long ago decided that Jesus Christ was my Lord and Savior, and I placed my life in his hands. With that in mind, I don't need a second opinion. I'm sure that Dr. Blumenthal got it right: I

CHARLES SLABAUGH

have cancer. I have decided not to seek or allow further treatment for my cancer. If God wants me to live, that's fine. If God wants me to die, I'm okay with that too."

With that, Ben sat down, and Father Gilbertson gave his final blessing to the group and announced, "The mass is ended. Go forth to bless and serve your fellow man."

That was our signal to leave. I wanted very much to speak with Ben, but he had quickly left the room with his CDs and the boom box. By the time I made my way to the outer room, the C/O in charge had already released us to return to our living units, so there was no way to speak with Ben.

Living in different living units with Stillwater's system of controlled movement meant it was a full week before I saw Ben again, and it was actually several weeks before I had a chance to speak with him face-to-face. That opportunity came Sundays three later when I got to the chapel for mass and caught up with Ben in the storage room again. Not knowing what to say, I opened with "Hi, Ben, how's it going?"

He flashed a quick smile. "Fine, I'm just fine. I'm glad to be here today, and I feel okay."

Knowing how short a time we had to visit, I got right to the point. "I've been thinking about you, Ben. I am very concerned about your decision to decline all treatment for your cancer problem. It's your business, I know, but I'm worried about you."

Again, with a smile, Ben said, "Thanks for your concern, but I know it's a good decision. I'm a lifer, I'm never going to get out of prison, alive. Long ago, I accepted that fact as an absolute certainty and right after I accepted Jesus Christ as Lord and Savior, and I decided to live my life for him, regardless. I did some awful things as a young man, that's why I'm a lifer. My life is his, and I accept whatever comes to me."

"That's all good and fine," I began, "but don't you think God wants us to avail ourselves of any and all medical help that is available to us?"

Still smiling, Ben said, "I know that I have cancer and will probably die from it. I'm comfortable with that, but waiting all those weeks and weeks to go somewhere to take tests or whatever was very hard on me. I accepted being in prison long ago. I don't fight this system, but to live in limbo – waiting for them to decide to send me at a time and place of their choosing – was really upsetting me . . ."

At that moment, Father Gilbertson stuck his head in the doorway. "Are we ready, Ben?"

Ben said, "Sure," and we all headed into the main room for mass.

As we were leaving after mass, Ben came over and said, "I'm really okay, and I'm completely comfortable with his will."

In the months that followed, I saw Ben weekly; from that vantage, little seemed to change. He seemed to look normal, his smile remained warm, and his rich deep tenor voice was unchanged. After a year or so, I noticed his gait seemed slower and less smooth, but whenever I spoke with him, he reported all was well. Best of all, his smile and warm, friendly attitude never wavered.

Then came a Sunday when Ben failed to show up for mass. Like many there, I immediately noticed his absence, and I wondered and worried as to the cause. At the end of the mass, Father Gilbertson made a short announcement: "Ben Simonton couldn't be with us today. He has been having some pain recently, and it is harder for him to move around. He has rescinded his formal refusal of treatment. He is now on 'special duty' at the Oak Park Heights medical unit. I saw him there yesterday. His spirits are good, and he will be going to the hospital soon for a complete evaluation. Please remember Ben in your prayers."

The next Sunday Ben was again absent, but the following Sunday he was back, and his smile was bright. At the end of the mass, Father Gilbertson said, "Ben has an announcement."

"All of my tests last week showed that my cancer has spread into my midsection and that it has invaded my bones. I received good care and treatment at Oak Park Heights and at the hospital. The doctors agreed that the disease can't be removed, but I have agreed to treat it to slow the spread and to manage the pain. Please understand I believe that if we believe in Christ as Lord and Savior, we must accept all things. I look forward to serving you here for many more Sundays. God bless you all."

With that, Father made his blessing and dismissed us.

Ben continued to enhance Christian services for many more years at Stillwater. His hair turned grayer, his stance grew less straight and true, and when I last saw him in person, he was walking slowly, leaning heavily on a cane as he navigated through the prison. Several times he resisted offers to relocate himself to the medical unit at Oak Park Heights, preferring to stay at Stillwater, a place he

CHARLES SLABAUGH

knew very well. His Minncor bosses were kind, allowing him to keep his clerk's job and its better income stream and also allowing Ben to take afternoons off on days when the morning routine had fatigued him. Ben was very sick, and he was still in prison, but he was doing it as much his way as anyone could inside Stillwater.

Chapter 14

A New Walking Partner

One of the hardest things about being in prison for me was the few opportunities we had to get outside and enjoy the sun. Inside prisons like Stillwater, if you had a job in the industry area, you got to take a short walk outside four times a day as you went to and from your assignment in the morning and in the afternoon. During most of my time at Stillwater, I worked in the Education Department. The Education Building, an old building that had been converted, rebuilt, from what had once been Stillwater's auditorium, was connected to the main corridor. The result was that you were never outside as you walked to and from work every day.

That made trips to the main yard the only option to see the sun or enjoy Mother Nature. During the months when we operated on summer time, we had more opportunities to visit the main yard, usually twice a day. In the winter, with short days the rule, we only had one chance to go to the main yard on Saturday and one chance on Sunday. Those yard periods were from forty-five minutes to a full hour on the planned schedule. I did my best to take advantage of every yard period offered.

Stillwater's main yard is a large open area in the prison's center, with the main complex of buildings on two sides and the prison's north wall on one side and a high chain-link fence topped with razor wire on the industry (west) side. Inside the yard was a large grassy field, with a softball diamond and a soccer field, plus a large area where touch football was played, all in the middle of things. On the sides, there were many basketball hoops and several handball courts. The grass-covered field in the center was surrounded by a hard-surfaced track, with running and walking lanes of almost a quarter mile in length. The track's walking lane was my favorite place to exercise and enjoy the outside whenever I could get there.

143

CHARLES SLABAUGH

As with almost all activities at Stillwater, we went to and from the main yard as a group in a formal, announced movement from our living area. Once in the yard, men quickly headed for their favorite activity, with me immediately entering the walking lane of the track. I was always anxious to see how many laps I could cram into the period. Sometimes I was joined by or would pair up with a friend, but I often walked alone. Walking solo was fine with me; my life's work had entailed many countless hours behind the wheel, driving alone. I was comfortable with my own company.

One winter day, as I rapidly circled the yard, enjoying a typical Minnesota winter day, a blue sky, almost cloudless with a bright yellow sun, and a cold breeze from the northwest, I was very much in my own thoughts. I was enjoying the day and my walk very much when an older man of small size and sporting an enormous beard fell in step with me. This was not uncommon on the track, and with typical prison behavior, we pretty much ignored each other for a lap or two. As an experienced walker, I set a rapid pace that some found difficult to match, but it was quickly obvious that my small silent companion was having no problem matching my stride. After a few minutes, I introduced myself with a short "I'm Chuck. Nice day, isn't it?"

He quickly answered, "I'm Max, you're pretty good at this." He then went on, "I just got here from Faribault. MCF – Faribault was a huge medium-security prison in Southern Minnesota. He went on, "I was here years ago, before all this controlled-movement stuff. It was better then."

At that point, the PA system announced the end of the period with its announcement, "The yard is closed. Get your IDs and all your personal property and head for the door. The yard is closed."

We finished our lap and headed back into the complex and back to our unit.

At that point, I was again living in D hall, the living unit I had briefly lived in when I had first arrived at Stillwater. Every year or so, the prison's administration rearranged the way that the inmate population was organized and moved us around. The most recent move had put many portions of the education group back into D house. I soon saw my recent walking partner, Max, walking around the unit. When I passed him on the flag, I said, "Hi, Max."

He said "hell-o" with a blank look on his face. Shortly after that, I ran into my friend Dale Bishop on the D house flag. Dale had a new job as a mentor to a small group of men with mental challenges. Run by the professionals of Psychology Department, this group operated under the label of "special needs group" and contained about twenty men who had trouble going through the daily Stillwater routine without direction or assistance. As Dale explained it, these men had one or more problems prohibiting them from a regular work or school assignment. Dale and a second friend, Ned Johns, were working as mentors to half of the group. They helped their charges with just about everything, from letter writing to remembering to brush their teeth or getting into the movement for lunch. They had divided their ten-man group in half, with each of them taking primary responsibility for five special needs inmates.

As Dale explained the group to me, he mentioned several of the group's members by name. One man I knew quite well from school years before, Omar Oogolala. He also mentioned Maxwell Larson. I asked, "Is he an older little guy with a big beard?"

Dale said, "Yes, that's Max. He loves to walk, but many of the younger guys are unkind to him because of his memory problems. They think he's dumb."

"What memory problems?" I asked.

"The problem is that Max has virtually no short-term memory. Max has Alzheimer's disease, and it's pretty bad. He was at Faribault in the Linden Unit (a special unit inside MCF – Faribault for older men with health issues), but he just couldn't do it. He kept missing meals and appointments. They sent him back here. The hope is that the controlled-movement system will help him keep organized. Max is a lifer, and he's never getting out. They're just trying to figure out the best place for him to be. He has no family that cares about him, so we're all he's got."

With Dale's explanation, I now understood Max's blank look when I had said "hi" earlier in the day. He hadn't remembered me. A few days later, on the main yard's track, Max again fell in step with me. I said, "Hi, Max."

He said, "Hell-o," and off we went around the track.

For the next almost two years, we walked together often until I was moved out of D hall in yet another reassortment of the inmate population.

In all the time that we walked together, we had basically the same conversation over and over. I'd be on the track, and Max would join me. In all that time, he never did remember my name but seemed confident that I was a friend or at least not an adversary. We would say or nod "Hell-o" and then do a lap or two. Soon Max would tell me that he was a welder and a toolmaker. He would continue, "When they set up the welding shops here years ago, I made all the forms."

CHARLES SLABAUGH

Max would always tell me that he was a Catholic, and I would say that I knew that because I always saw him at the Sunday morning mass every week.

As Max could remember almost nothing, I often wondered how he got to early Catholic Sunday mass. To get to any religious service or meeting at Stillwater, inmates had to sign up on a posted notice several days in advance of the service. If you had signed up, the morning of the service, meeting, or event, you would find an individual movement pass on your door's bars when you woke up in the morning. The pass, made out in your name, would list the event, its scheduled time, and its location. If you failed to sign up on the posted notice, you would never get the pass, and in Stillwater's system, you couldn't go anywhere individually without a pass.

One day Dale Bishop explained to me, like many Alzheimer's patients, Max was always walking somewhere. D house was shaped like a U, with a two-sided cellblock, and Max spent many hours each day drifting around the flag. Somehow he had learned the critical importance of the sign-up sheets, and every time he passed the bulletin board with those sheets hanging on it, he would see what was being offered. If the service or event was of interest, he would check to see if his name was already on the form. If it was not there yet, he would sign up. I'm sure Max must have checked those sheets fifty times some days, but he always went to mass. I was amazed at his determination and perseverance.

Money, always an issue in prison, was another problem for Max. He had no outside assistance and no longer could work for income, but members of the special needs group received about $30 a month for being in the group and attending its meetings. To find out how much money each of us in Stillwater had in our account, we would run our ID tag through a swipe terminal in the gym. Max went to the gym twice daily, and he would swipe his card every time he walked by the terminal. Unfortunately, he couldn't remember the balance, no matter how many times he saw it flash. In this situation, and in many others, his mentor Dale Bishop helped. Dale would make a point to look over Max's shoulder when he swiped his ID card. Then on the day we turned in Canteen orders, Dale would visit Max in his cell and help him decide what to order and to budget his meager funds. Just like working with a child, Dale would inventory Max's things, pointing out the need for a new bar of soap, a bottle of laundry detergent, writing paper, etc., and also trying to keep the inventory of candy bars (Max's favorite snack) under control.

Sometimes thoughtless fellow inmates were not the only ones giving Max a hard time. One morning, as I was returning to D hall from a pass, Max was going out the door with an older female sergeant letting him out just as I approached the main hall's metal detector. As you entered the main hall from the D hall door, you

A DEGREE FOR HENRY

had to turn either right or left, depending on your destination. I knew this small decision was always a huge problem for Max. With his Alzheimer's disease, he couldn't remember where anyplace was, and he was always stymied at this point. From his blank, confused expression, it was obvious that he didn't know which way to turn. It was also obvious that the sergeant was not in a good mood. When Max said, "Where do I go?" she snapped back, "Oh, you'll figure it out!" And she closed and locked the door behind him, leaving him clueless in the hall.

I went through the metal detector and crossed over to the door, said, "How's it going, Max?"

He replied, "Where am I going?"

I reached over and took the pass from his hand. Reading the pass, Max was heading for a meeting in the chapel, a room he had visited hundreds, maybe thousands, of times over the years. I said, "You're going to the chapel for a group meeting, Max. Go to the right, and when you get to the end of the hall, at the next set of metal detectors, turn left. It's right there."

His reply was a concise "Okay."

He started in that direction, and I said, "Hey, Max, don't forget the metal detector," pointing to the machine across the hall from us.

"Oh yeah," he muttered, changing direction to the machine.

I watched him move down the hall for a minute to make sure he was moving in the right way, and then I rapped on the D hall door.

The female sergeant opened the door, and as I walked in, she said, "The old fool acts like he can't remember just to get attention. You know, he killed a brother officer of mine, a Duluth City policeman."

I nodded in her direction, marveling that anyone could really believe that Max could so perfectly carry out such a charade, but I think she really believed that Max was just pretending a memory problem.

Max quickly became my regular walking partner. He was always quick to comment on the weather, and he always told me of his work as a welder and toolmaker. He never called me by my name because he couldn't remember it, but somehow he knew I was a friend or at least not an adversary. He would frequently comment on his health, saying it was good, but then he would add, "I do okay at just about everything except remembering."

When I asked him about his family, his mind was clear, remembering in detail his early life in Pennsylvania, a family of brothers and sisters, a wife (long-ago divorced), and a daughter. He remembered where several siblings lived, some still in Pennsylvania and a sister in Arizona. He said his daughter had for a long time been in touch, but at this point in his life, there was no one in touch as far as he could recall. As we circled Stillwater's yard, he told me about his early years at Stillwater, and he remembered being at Oak Park Heights, a close-by supermax prison. He remembered being at MCF – Faribault, and he remembered liking things there. When I asked why he had left Faribault, he grew confused and quiet.

One day, as I crossed the flag in front of D hall's inmate barbershop, a converted cell, Dale Bishop called to me from inside the shop. He had Max in the barber's chair, and there seemed to be a problem. I knew that Dale frequently helped out the men in the special needs group with haircuts. He wasn't really a barber, but he was a very competent amateur. For many inmates with their small income, getting a decent haircut at Stillwater was nearly impossible. Cell hall barbers were paid as swampers. In theory, haircuts were free to all, but the free cut was usually the 1950s-style butch. To get anything else required a substantial tip of Canteen goods to the barber. For many of those men, Dale Bishop was a huge help. He offered free haircuts, asking only that the inmate visit the chapel on Sunday.

I was surprised to see Max in the chair. Max always needed a haircut and beard trim, but he seemed very content being unkempt and untrimmed, yet here he was in the chair with a nylon drape over his torso.

Dale quickly but quietly explained that every few months, he tried to get Max in the chair for a trimming, but today Max was unhappy with the process. Dale wanted me to join the small party and visit with Max. He thought that would distract Max, and I agreed to the ruse. I quickly started, "Hi, Max. How's it going today?"

He answered, "I'm okay, but this guy wants to cut my hair. I don't need a haircut, do I?"

I replied, "Well, Max, you've certainly got a lot of hair. I would guess that you would be more comfortable with some of it trimmed away. You know, summer is coming, and these old buildings get pretty hot. Why don't you let Dale take a bit of it off?"

A DEGREE FOR HENRY

"Okay," he replied.

With that, Dale started to trim, and I stood in front of Max, trying to keep him occupied. It really wasn't hard, and we were soon into our yard conversation, with Max telling me of welding, making tools, and growing up in Pennsylvania.

At one point, Max mentioned that he was never getting out of prison because he had killed a cop. At that, Dale asked, "How did that happen?"

Max's answer was right in character. "I don't know," he stated, "but he must have made me mad. I have a very bad temper."

I had to take his word for that. In all the time I knew Max, I never saw him be anything but quiet, calm, and confused.

Chapter 15

A New Man

Early on, during my brief career as a DOC woodworker, I met Paul Rasmusson. Paul was a native of rural Minnesota, who, over twenty years before, had found himself in a California prison serving a "life without the possibility of parole" sentence. After serving twenty-plus years in various California prisons, in the process of which he had received a second "life without" sentence for committing the murder of another inmate inside of prison (a crime the system referred to as an institutional murder), he was transferred to the Minnesota system, still serving his California sentences.

Paul was transferred under an interstate compact agreement, under which member states can move inmates from one state to another. These moves can be made to get a prisoner closer to his family, to accommodate one state's prison system seeking to rid themselves of a problem inmate, or to remove an inmate when he is no longer safe where he is.

Paul was a formidable presentation: 6 feet 2 inches, 275 pounds, complete with heavily-tattooed arms and neck, and countless stories of life in California's infamous prisons. I never knew him well, but there was no way not to notice him. He was loud, demanding, and assertive. After I had been working in education for several years, Paul took a tutor's job in another literacy classroom.

Despite the "without the possibility of parole" portion of his sentences, every few years, the California system would schedule inmates with such sentences for parole hearings. To the California DOC, the point was to check in with and up on the inmate and monitor how he was spending his time. To Paul Rasmusson, and almost universally to all men with similar sentences, these hearings represented

A DEGREE FOR HENRY

an opportunity to plead their case, hoping for release or at least for improvement in that direction. For Paul Rasmusson, whose total time of incarceration was approaching thirty years, the matter had become most urgent.

During his many years in prison in California and now in Minnesota, Rasmusson had worked a plethora of jobs, and he had participated in many programs, but as he prepared for a hearing in his twenty-eighth year of incarceration, it became painfully obvious to him that he could point to a very shallow pool of accomplishments as he labored to organize his presentation.

He had heard from other inmates that having earned college credits and degrees was a positive, persuasive thing to many parole boards, but he had not done so. He had taken some classes over the years, but they had not led to a degree, and at this point, he didn't even have detailed information as to which course he had completed or what grades he had earned. In fact, he hadn't completed several of the courses that he had started.

He also knew of inmates who had "found God" and were able to show a complete change of direction in their life at the hearing, but Paul hadn't been inside a church since he was a very young boy.

As he contemplated his dilemma, Rasmusson was working in one of Stillwater's many woodshops that produced furniture. With over twenty-eight years in prison, a boy rich in prison tattoo art and countless stories of life in California prisons, he had acquired a large group of admirers at Stillwater. He had also become quite active in Stillwater's main Aryan group, the PMBs. A group of white men, the PMBs advocated white power, and Paul Rasmusson soon became the group's president. The group's name, PMB, stood for Prison Motor Bike, and these men all considered themselves to be true "bikers"; much like Marlon Brando's portrayal of an outlaw biker in movies. The PMB name had stuck inside Stillwater, and these men loved the role.

Paul had decided to leave his woodshop job and to take a job in the Education Department. His goal was to take enough college work to complete a degree that he had started years before in California. Before he could put any of his plans into motion, he fell victim to a random urine analysis (UA) test.

One morning he was sent to the security center on a pass. When he arrived there, he found five of his PMB brothers also there and all of them being required to provide a urine sample. Members of the squad were present, administering the tests. All six inmates were told that they had been selected on a random basis. As the six of them had been drinking some new prison "hooch" the night before in

CHARLES SLABAUGH

their unit, A East, it was obvious to all involved that there was nothing "random" about any of this, but that's what the paperwork was stamped: RANDOM.

When all six inmates tested positive for alcohol, and two of them were also positive for pot, all six of them were quickly in handcuffs and on their way to segregation, the hole. After a meeting with the discipline sergeant, Paul agreed to sign for the charge, accepting a segregation sentence of thirty, do fifteen. For the next fifteen days, he sat in segregation, spending most of his awake time telling all who wanted to listen stories about his time in California's infamous Folsom Prison.

When he was finished with the segregation time, Paul was randomly sent to B West to spend the mandatory ninety days as a UI, an unemployed inmate. During this time, he was locked in his cell on the flag twenty-three hours per day. In addition to his mandatory one hour out of his cell daily, he went to meals with the unit in the dining hall. When he returned to B West after a meal, Paul and the other men on UI or TU status had to immediately switch in to their cell, while the men with assignments were allowed to use the workout machines, the card/game tables, or to just hang out on the flag.

For many of the men, the idle time was very hard: one is just sitting alone inside his cell, watching most of the rest of the unit playing cards, working out, using the phone, taking showers, walking around, or just hanging out. It wasn't as bad for Rasmusson as he often had a crowd of friends standing at his door, gossiping or listening to a new California prison story. His long open-ended sentences made him a celebrity to some of the inmates, especially to some of the younger men. Rasmusson was an old hand at manipulating other men, and he made the most of these opportunities. He presented himself as a victim of the system and of circumstance, and he cultivated his new admirers respect and devotion skillfully.

Rasmusson's arms and neck were covered with prison ink, tattoos from his many years in California's prison system. As he regaled his admirers with stories from those years, he was quick to point out his intricate spider web-patterned tattoos over each elbow. He would explain that those signified that he had killed mud people, as he called them, inside prison.

As much as he had become a bit of a hero to his young followers, what Rasmusson really wanted, desperately wanted, was release from prison. Despite his being in the Minnesota system, he was, in fact, a California prisoner, and the question of his release was completely a California decision.

A DEGREE FOR HENRY

During the time he was sitting out his ninety-day UI time, after his true segregation sentence was over, he came due for a periodic review of his case by the California parole board. Thanks to twenty-first-century technology, that would be handled almost effortlessly using a video conference via the Internet. As the date for the hearing drew close, Rasmusson was determined to present a good case and to obtain a positive outcome. For him, that meant release from prison.

He labored over the written presentation, which was actually a letter he would send to the board in advance of the hearing, stressing that he was a changed man and that he was now ready to rejoin society. His case was thin. He actually had accomplished little that was either positive or constructive, but he did his best to craft a favorable image of himself as having become a changed person.

The night before the hearing, he could not sleep. As hard as he tried, he could not slow down his brain as it raced through a conflicting collage of thoughts. Over and over, he went through what he was going to say to the board. That image was constantly interrupted with thoughts of what he would do if (*when*) he was free. He would catch himself as his mind digressed and force it to return to what he was going to say and exactly how he would say it. Before he knew it, he was thinking of being out and being able to do as he wished – to eat a big, thick steak; to have a beer (several beers); and to have a woman, yes, to feel the excitement of being with a warm, welcome, responding woman. Paul had a long, restless, uncomfortable night.

Like almost everyone inside of Stillwater, being with a woman was an enticing thought to Rasmusson. Early on in his California time, Rasmusson had been able to meet a woman who agreed to visit and to write to him, and ultimately, they were married. Under the rules then in force in California, they were even allowed conjugal visits and a child resulted, a son he named Paul Jr. Rasmusson had never seen the boy in the flesh. By the time the boy was born, his wife had become disillusioned, and she had lost interest in Paul. She stopped visiting, and she ultimately divorced him years ago.

Rasmusson had done his best to stay in touch, but with the limits on his ability to use the phone, and with her power to accept or to reject his calls, plus his almost complete dependence on her for money, there was little he could do once she became disenchanted.

When his son became eighteen years old, just a few years before, the boy had written to Rasmusson who was by then in Minnesota. Rasmusson had immediately written back, anxious to restore or create a bond with the boy and recruit a supporter. When he pressed Paul Jr. for some money to purchase new eyeglasses so that he wouldn't have to wear the extremely-unattractive glasses that the prison provided, the boy quit responding to his letters. At first, that angered Rasmusson. "How can he do that?" he thought. "I'm his father." Then Rasmusson caught himself. "What do I care about those damn glasses?" he thought. "I've got bigger things on my mind."

Rasmusson jerked awake, aware that he had been dreaming. "I've got to focus today," he thought angrily. "I've got to make sure that this hearing goes well. The board must understand that I'm a new, changed man who deserves another chance."

With that, he began to run through his presentation again. Any thought of sleep was abandoned.

Finally, it was morning, and he joined the movement to breakfast with most of B West. He really wasn't hungry, but he was awake with nothing to do until his hearing, which was scheduled for 2:00 PM Pacific time or noon in Minnesota.

After breakfast, a pathetic imitation of McDonald's famous Sausage McMuffin with Egg, Paul was back in his cell. He was determined to look his best today, despite the fact that they would see him only on a black-and-white TV image from the waist up, so he asked a passing C/O about a shower. "No" came the reply. "Not until your hour out at 2:30 PM."

"But I've got a parole hearing at noon, and I want to look good," Rasmusson pleaded.

The young C/O kept walking, saying, "Can't help you," over his disappearing shoulder.

Not allowing him a morning shower was not unexpected, and Rasmusson refused to allow it to bother him. Paul busied himself at the sink. He got his long hair in shape and set to work on his face. Like many in prison, he shaved about once a week as a rule, but this was a special day. He carefully scraped his face clean, taking off the chin whiskers that he had cultivated for months, determined to look clean-cut.

He then took a "bird bath" in the sink. Once he was as cleaned up as possible, he took a clean T-shirt out of his wardrobe and a new-looking pair of jeans.

The shirt and the blue jeans were brand new. Rasmusson had gotten a PMB buddy who worked in the Property Department to steal them and pass them to

A DEGREE FOR HENRY

him, using another buddy who was a B West swamper. Neither garment had ever been worn or washed, and Rasmusson had meticulously ironed them with sharp creases in them the day before during his hour out. He didn't put them on yet, fearful of wrinkling them. He laid them carefully on his bunk. For the rest of the morning, he sat in old but clean sweats, waiting for the lunch movement at 10:45. He didn't even turn on his TV but sat in his plastic chair, going over and over what he planned to say in his mind. He kept telling himself that "They needed to understand – they must understand – I'm a changed man!"

When B West was called for lunch, Paul wasn't even hungry, but he went anyway. Several friends, knowing that his hearing was today – hearing day – wished him well as they passed, giving him high-fives and good-luck messages as he went through the routine of lunch. Rasmusson gladly accepted their encouragement, responding with words that he hoped sounded confident. Inside, his stomach was churning and his nerves were knotting, but he didn't want anyone to see that. He was determined to appear calm and confident – very cool. This was going to be his day.

At 11:25, he dressed in his clean, ironed T-shirt and jeans, expecting to be taken to the video conference room before the noon count, when a C/O arrived at his door. "California just e-mailed, they are running late," he began. "They have rescheduled you for 4:20 their time, 2:20 our time. You'll stay here for count. We'll come get you about 1:40 and get you out of here before the 2:00 watch change."

Rasmusson was numb for a moment and then said, "That's cutting it pretty close to the watch change, isn't it?"

"No" came the reply. "We'll have lots of time."

Rasmusson could only sit there and worry. "Now what else can go wrong?"

Before he could speak, the C/O walked on. In desperation and frustration, Paul turned on his TV, seeking diversion. Sadly, daytime TV had little to offer.

Count seemed to last forever, but it finally cleared by the PA system. Soon movements were announced for education and for a group of men with passes for the library. Paul continued to sit and wait, going over his presentation and praying that his stomach would settle down. And 1:40 came and went, but no one came for him. He began to panic mentally. *They have forgotten me* was him lament, but suddenly, the C/O, keys in hand, was at his door.

"Did you think that I forgot you?" was his question.

CHARLES SLABAUGH

Rasmusson did his best to smile and mumble a "no."

Rapidly, Rasmusson walked to the B West door, out onto the main corridor, and then west toward the video conference room. Rasmusson's mind was a mess, racing over his presentation and then to thoughts of freedom and all that it implied. He knew that he absolutely had to get this right.

When he entered the video conference room next to the security center, a C/O directed him to a chair at a small table. On the table sat a small monitor with a camera on top pointed back at him. The C/O explained to Paul that he would be able to see and hear the California parole and pardons board on the screen, and that they would also be able to see him; all in real time.

Filled with excitement, emotion, and dread simultaneously, Rasmusson asked, "Do I begin with my statement?"

The C/O answered, "Maybe. They are in charge. Let them tell you what the plan is."

Before he could reply, the screen flickered and fluttered, coming to life. Rasmusson could see a fairly-clear image or a large room with a long table in the center. Seven people sat at that table facing him. They were seated in large high-backed upholstered chairs. Rasmusson thought they looked like judges in a courtroom, although he couldn't see their faces easily and no one wore a judge's robe. A voice from the screen said, "Hell-o, is this Ohio?"

Rasmusson didn't know what to say, but the C/O leaned in and said, "No, this is Stillwater Prison in Minnesota. Are you ready for us?"

A voice from the screen said, "Minnesota? I thought we were doing Rostov in Ohio now."

Another voiced from the screen said, "No, Minnesota is next. Is that you, Mr. Rasmusson?"

Relieved to hear his name, Rasmusson said, "Yes, this is Paul Rasmusson. May I begin with my statement?"

Another screen voice, this one female, said, "We're way off schedule already, and we have reviewed your case and the reports of your time in Minnesota. As you know, you are serving two separate 'life without the possibility of parole' sentences, one that sent you to prison and one that came from an institutional

A DEGREE FOR HENRY

murder inside prison. We see that you are doing your time, and there has not been another charge brought in court since the murder that gave you the second sentence." With that, the screen went blank.

Paul Rasmusson had experienced the horror that had become reality in California's huge, impersonal prison system. While life in Minnesota wasn't pleasant or enjoyable, it was definitely better. The living units were smaller and less chaotic. He could still live pretty much as he wished. Minnesota was, he had no doubt, a better place to be incarcerated than California.

During the next two weeks, Paul continued to sit out his ninety days of enforced unemployment. Rasmusson thought over his situation and brooded. His several PMB buddies in the unit were frequent visitors to his door. They were all sympathetic, agreeing how completely unfair his situation was. Some suggested that he ought to "sue the bastards" to force a parole. Paul absolutely agreed that this was unfair. "That two-minute hearing was completely bogus!"

He also understood the realities of his situation. His parents were old and retired on a small income. They sent him what money they could, but they couldn't even come for visits from their farm in Southern Minnesota. Lately, they were even writing less often, and the rest of his family had dropped out of his life years before. The woman he had married when he was first in prison had lost interest and divorced him. His son, the product of California's now-discontinued policy of conjugal visits, had written a few years before, seeking to establish a bond or at least a link to his father. When Rasmusson had responded with an appeal for money, none came, and his son never wrote again. "No," he thought. "I'm going to have to do this 100 percent by myself. I am about as alone as a guy can be. I'm sure glad that I have friends in here!"

As the slow weeks without a job passed, Paul developed a strategy. It was obvious to him that the people in charge had pretty much written him off. If he was going to ever get their attention in a positive way, he was going to have to change himself or at least what they saw in him. They obviously thought education was a good thing, and they gave at least lip service to God. Paul decided that he would become what they liked. He would go to college and actually complete a degree. He wasn't sure how hard that would be, but he resolved to do it, regardless of how hard the work was.

The second part of the strategy would be harder. He resolved to become a churchgoing Christian, regardless of how difficult or painful that would be. In all his years in prison, the only times he had attended a church service was to meet another inmate, using the pretense of worship to overcome the controlled-movement system. Now he was going to get very involved with religion.

To help make both changes, Paul got his head together with his PMB buddies, explaining what he was about to do. They were surprised but quickly understood his dilemma. Paul was fifty-two years, old and he had been in prison for almost thirty years. If he was ever to get out – and even he admitted that was far from certain – he had to show these people that he had changed, really changed.

Once he had cleared his plan with the PMBs, Paul quickly got a kite off to Stanley Marcus, the man in charge of higher-education classes inside Stillwater. Stan Marcus quickly responded with a pass for a meeting. At their meeting, he quickly explained the program to Paul. Stillwater was working with a small Twin Cities community college, arranging courses that led to an AA degree. While the small community college was facilitating the program, the faculty was hired on paper as adjunct professors by Augsburg College in Minneapolis. Augsburg, a small well-rated Lutheran college, then awarded the credits and any resulting degrees. Stan Marcus emphasized to Paul Rasmusson that an Augsburg degree was a prestigious award.

Paul quickly said, "No way. I want a four-year BA degree."

Stan Marcus agreed that was a worthwhile goal, but Minnesota's legislature would not underwrite the cost of a BA for an inmate. Further, he pointed out that Paul was too old and had the wrong crime(s) to be eligible for federal funding. Stan Marcus said Paul would need to earn an AA degree in the Stillwater program. Then if he could, he might finish the four-year degree completely at his own expense. Marcus said that he could be helpful in communicating with teachers, etc., and Rasmusson could probably use the computer lab, but he would have to bear the cost of tuition, books, etc., personally for the final two years of the four-year program.

Paul Rasmusson accepted that bad news quietly, almost stoically. He had assumed that this would be hard; everything was hard in prison.

The next Sunday morning he got up early, and for the first time in his many years in prison, he found a pass for the morning chapel service on his bars. He was extremely self-conscious as he entered the chapel, and many of the men already in their seats were amazed when he entered the room and took a seat.

Going to chapel services was a key ingredient in Paul Rasmusson's strategy to secure a parole from the California system. He had concluded that the parole

A DEGREE FOR HENRY

board seemed intent on seeing evidence of real change in the men they chose for release and that educational accomplishments and seeing a person move toward God seemed to get their approval. Paul was very nervous about the second portion of his plan – the part about appearing to become religious. All his life, he had held religious people in low esteem, frequently belittling them and calling them names to their face. Paul was convinced that highly-religious people were really weak and unable to accomplish much by themselves. In his mind, religion was the fallback position of the weak and timid, and Paul Rasmusson was neither weak nor timid. Over his many years in prison, time and again, he had proven his strength and boldness. Now he was going to present himself as just exactly what he was not: a quiet, contemplative, religious man. This was going to be hard, but he was determined to escape from prison via the parole system. He was determined not to end up as an old man and die in prison. "Not me!" he vowed.

The previous week he had met with the other men who were leaders of the PMBs, Stillwater's dominant Aryan gang, and explained his plan. When Paul had first arrived at Stillwater, he had quickly sought out and met with the PMB leadership. By rights of his reputation and status with the Aryan leadership in the California system, Paul was immediately accepted as a member, and he immediately became a leader of the Stillwater PMBs. Paul's second "life without parole" sentence was a direct result of an institutional murder he had participated in at California's Folsom Prison. The victim was Hispanic, member of a rival gang. That alone qualified him for membership, respect, and honor by Stillwater's PMBs. Paul had expected such homage, and he was soon the group's president. In the strange, often-conflicted world of prison, Rasmusson was the president of a group that didn't officially exist. In fact, his very membership in the group would send him to segregation if it became known. It was, indeed, a strange world.

Now he was divesting himself of all such trappings of membership and leadership. As he explained, "You know that I'm with you 100 percent. My heart and soul is with you forever, but I've got to get a parole, and to get that done, I have to look lily white to that fucking parole board."

All understood and agreed; effective immediately, a new president was chosen, and Paul completely dropped out of active, obvious participation in the Stillwater PMG group.

His first time in chapel went well too. He was surprised when several of the inmate leaders of the chapel Christians welcomed him with smiles and welcoming handshakes. He quickly noticed that most attending had brought along a personal Bible. Paul had never owned a Bible. As a boy, his mother had a Bible, but he had never needed one. He was thinking about that as he sat and waited for the service

CHARLES SLABAUGH

to begin when Dale Bishop handed him a paperbound Bible. Bishop said, "This will help you follow what we are doing this morning. They are free to all. You may take it with you, if you wish." With that, the outside volunteers who had gathered at the front of the room started the service with a hymn. Dale came over again, handing Paul a blue hymnal, saying, "It's number 316."

Paul quickly turned to the page. Then noticing that everyone else was standing up, he rose and joined the singing.

The service was not what he had expected, but actually, Paul hadn't known what to expect. He hadn't been to a church since he was a little boy, and his grandmother had taken him to the small Baptist church near her farm. At one point, two inmates had stood up and individually spoken of how God had changed their lives. The idea of doing that made Paul uncomfortable, but no one called on him to do anything; much to his relief.

When the service ended and they were waiting in the chapel's entrance area for the C/O to release them, Paul still had the paperbound Bible in his hand. Dale Bishop came by again and said, "The Bible is yours, if you want it. If you ever want to purchase a nicer one, I have a good catalog you may use anytime. I hope you will come again. You are very welcome here."

As he shook Dale's hand, all Paul could think to say was "Okay, I'm Rasmusson."

With that, the C/O in charge announced the movement, and they all headed out of the chapel and through the main hall's metal detector and then back to their respective living units.

Later, as Rasmusson thought about the service, he concluded, "I can do this. I'll show those assholes on the parole board that I deserve a parole. I'll earn a college degree, and I'll look like Jesus Christ himself."

Three days later, when Paul returned to his cell after his hour out, he found an envelope on the cell's floor marked "Official Business, Board of Pardons and Parole" addressed to him. He knew from experience what it was: his formal, written notice from the parole board of the outcome of his hearing, signed by all members of the parole board. It was the official determination from the hearing. He was correct; it was precisely that pro forma paperwork. What he was unprepared for were the words written under the chair's signature in the same pen as the chair's signature. The message was succinct and clear: "We said Life, and we meant Life!"

A DEGREE FOR HENRY

For a very long time, Paul Rasmusson sat staring at the words. Almost anyone else in prison would have at least considered giving up any hope or dream of eventual release, but such was not the case with Paul. Suddenly wadding up the ugly message, he tossed it in his waste can, and with both fists clenched tightly together, he thought, "Fuck him, fuck all of them, I'll show them. I'll look like the perfect picture of a new man. They won't be able to refuse me next time."

With that, he slammed his cell's door shut, turned on his overhead light, and prepared for the afternoon standing count.

Chapter 16

NEW DIRECTION AND A NEW GOAL

With Stillwater's controlled-movement system, only one group (living unit) could change locations at one time. That meant that for the beginning of the school day, the tutors came to work ten to fifteen minutes before the students arrived as the two groups lived in different units. The entire education group was Stillwater's largest, and because of its size, it was spread over parts of four living units. That gave the tutors a small amount of time every morning for preparations before the students arrived.

One morning Donald Jergens sat down at Jane's desk and brought her up-to-date on his student's progress, and he also updated her on the evening poetry group's activities. Don wanted Jane to know who was doing well, who was not, and why. He wanted Jane to know how well he felt Omar Oogolala was doing in the poetry group. "His spelling and grammar are still very rough, but I think he's going to really do himself some good," said Donald, summing up his report.

"How about you?" Jane replied.

A bit confused, Don stammered, "Me?"

Jane continued, "Don, I've been watching you. You have made so much progress since you first came here. You are bright, your mind is quick and curious, but it seems that you are not interested in going beyond your GED. I can't understand why you'd just stop. We offer college classes here three times a year. They cost you almost nothing - $5 for an entire 4- credit-hour class. I think you should be all over us to get enrolled. Aren't you interested?"

A DEGREE FOR HENRY

"Well, ma'am," Don began, "I guess I never saw myself as college material. My mother and my elder sister went to college – they're both teachers – but I never thought it was for me. Now that I've come to prison, I can never be a teacher like they are, so . . ."

"Maybe yes, maybe no," Jane snapped. "Don, the point is you have a good mind. I think – I know – that you can do this. You're going to be in prison for a long time, why not make the most of that time? In our staff meeting yesterday, Ms. Polinski said we have classes beginning next month. She's looking for students. Please think about it. If you're interested, you can get back to me, or you can send Ms. Polinski a kite yourself. Now here come the students, but please think about this. College would be a good thing for you."

Don did think it over that day and through the evening. The next morning he told Jane, "I'm interested. What do I do now?"

"I'll make a call," replied a beaming Jane Halverson.

Twenty minutes later, she handed Don a pass to speak with Mr. Marcus who coordinated the higher-education effort inside Stillwater. When Don got to his office on the first floor of the Education Building, Stan Marcus showed him a listing of four classes scheduled in the next semester. One of the classes was a special course for men with no college experience. It offered only 2 credit hours toward the college degree, but Mr. Marcus suggested that Don take it to help get his feet on the ground. Don agreed and asked, "Should I just take one class?"

Mr. Marcus's suggestion was to select maybe one more course from the choices of cultural anthropology, statistics, and creative writing. Don chose creative writing. He knew he could be creative.

The next few months were a complete revelation to Don. He learned how to do college research, how to write a term paper, how to take notes, and Don learned a lot about himself. None of it was easy, but once he got going, it was as if he had found a new way of life. It wasn't nearly as difficult as Don had anticipated.

The biggest revelation to Don was that he had talent, that he really could write and express himself creatively. Through his poetry, he had often achieved noticed by being provocative – by saying things using language that assaulted the reader's sense of propriety. Now Don learned that he could capture a reader's attention with ideas. This pleased and excited him, but it also gratified his deep buried desire to call attention to the many injustices he saw in daily life inside Stillwater.

CHARLES SLABAUGH

Before he realized it, the semester was ending. For a final exercise, each creative writing student was to write a major work – a super paper. The teacher, a lady from a college in Northfield, Minnesota, whom Don found inspiring, specified neither a minimum nor a maximum length for the work. Instead, she told them to identify an injustice in their daily life. They were to identify the problem or issue, explain why it was an excellent example of an absolute wrong, and then present a solution. They were to use only the number of words necessary, no more and no less.

After a great deal of thought, Don decided that standardized testing represented an injustice to many students. In his paper, Don explained the problem and how it unfairly penalized students with deficient language skills, those with learning disabilities, and also to those who were in the ESL (English as a second language) category. His solution was for each student to be evaluated individually. What delighted his teacher was that Don didn't just leave the issue there; he went on to point out that his solution would result in a major increase in school staffing to personally evaluate so many students and then monitor the results of so much analysis. Don went on to postulate how, in the long run, his solution would save money and serve society better. In his model, in the end, society would actually spend less and come out with a better-educated population.

The instructor was delighted with his identification of the issue and even more so with his creative and inventive solution, giving his ninety-eight-page paper a grade of A+. That gave Don a grade of A- in the course. He also earned an A in the college skills course.

Don was overwhelmed. He had always feared that he couldn't do college work. Now he had taken two college-level courses, and he had an A average. When he received a note of congratulations from Ms. Polinski, the education director, he was amazed and thrilled. A few days later, he received a pass to visit Norma Kolkins, the lady who ran the college Spector program. The receipt of that pass caused him concern and confusion. What was wrong now, what had he done, was all that he could wonder.

Later that day in Norma's office, she was quick to get to the point. "Seldom," she began, "have I seen a beginning student in a demanding class like Shirley Dombroski's creative writing do so well. Several years ago, a student in a similar situation of beginning college work was simply overwhelmed with the course." Don was thrilled and excited. He told her the truth, that he found the course exciting and rewarding. "Well," Norma went on, "that's why I asked you to come in. I hoped your reply would be that positive. We'd like you to join the Spector group and become a full-time student. We have too few really-committed students, and your instructors think that you can go on to earn your AA college degree here at Stillwater." Don was relieved and excited but quickly brought up the subject of the evening poetry group. Smiling, Norma said, "Jane said you'd want to continue that. It's all set. You can continue with that program, and I'll include those hours with your Spector pay plan. You'll get a little extra money for those hours."

No one in prison ever had enough money, and Don quickly agreed. Much to his amazement, he was on his way, so it seemed, to a college education inside Stillwater's cold, dark walls.

Chapter 17

Disaster

It was finally Friday afternoon, and most inmates were relaxing in anticipation of a weekend off. Many would catch up on their sleep, enjoy some time in the gym or yard, or wash clothes. Many men received visits from friends or family on the weekends. Visiting was open Thursday, Friday, Saturday, and Sunday, but the busiest days were Saturday and Sunday. Everyone was anticipating a break from their normal routine.

Right after supper, the PA system began calling men to the bubble, B West's fully-enclosed administrative center, where the sergeant or the OIC (officer in charge) ran the unit. Located midway in the unit on the flag, the bubble was elevated several feet above the ground level, so those inside had a clear view of the flag and all of B West's eight tiers. The PA system kept calling men's names, and one-by-one, they went down to the bubble, approaching the built-in microphone and announcing themselves. Curious as to what was going on, I walked out onto the tier's catwalk and watched the unfolding drama. I lived on the back half of the third tier – the 700s of the unit's numbering system – and I had a clear view of the show.

As each man identified himself, the large sliding drawer in the bubble's side wall would open and extend out. This drawer was like the drawer one encounters at many bank drive-in windows. Each inmate would then reach into the drawer and remove several sheets of paper. Watching them as they read the papers, it was obvious that they were not getting good news. Some just jammed the papers in a pocket and walked off, but several men displayed great anger. Some wadded the paper up and threw them down onto the flag's floor. In one case, a young man tore the papers into small pieces and threw them up in the air as he stalked off, obviously very upset.

When Henry Jimenez's name was called, it hit me. I turned to Steve Kline who had joined me at the rail and said, "Those are all Spector guys."

"Yeah," Steve agreed, "and those pink sheets they are all getting are program-termination notices. I don't know what has happened, but this is going to be a mess."

As we stood there, more names were called, and the show at the bubble went on and on.

Soon Henry returned to the tier, and Steve asked him, "What's the deal?"

"The letter says we were cheating," Henry said. "The letter says we cheated on the Math for Liberal Arts midterm. We are all getting an F for the course. We are all terminated from the Spector program. Those assholes are throwing us out of everything for just one stupid test in a fucking course that nobody was getting. It's all just another piece of shit!"

With that, Henry quickly went into his cell, closing the door behind him.

Steve Kline walked over to Henry's door and said, "What did you guys do?"

Henry's answer was "What do you think? No one was getting that stuff. We had to do something. There was just too much at stake to let our futures go down the drain for one dumb math class." He then added, "We got a copy of the test and its answer sheet, and we all memorized the answers. I guess we got the wrong one because they got on to us because we all got the same wrong answers, and now twenty-three of us are out of the program." Steve opened Henry's door and went into his cell. Henry was despondent in the extreme, and as the evening went on, his mood darkened more and more. "This is the worst thing that has ever happened in my life" was his first statement, and that was his theme for the rest of the evening. "I will never get a college degree. All my plans are destroyed, all because of that stupid class."

Steven immediately countered, "No, the worst thing that ever happened in your life was coming to prison. We can fix this. You'll be out of school for a bit, but we can get you back in the program fairly quickly. I'll talk to Ms. Polinski. She's a fair person . . ."

CHARLES SLABAUGH

"I tried to talk to her this morning!" Henry yelled. "I passed that bitch on my way out of the Education Building after the math teacher told us all that he knew we had all cheated. She said, 'Oh, Henry, what a mess,' and then she waved me off. She wouldn't even listen to me. The whole fucking course was ridiculous with that asshole teacher from Africa. No one could understand him or his math."

Steven said, "She was upset. This will cause her a lot of grief and make her look bad, but Pam's a realist too. Once this blows over, and a little time passes, we can get you back in school. All this really means is a bit of delay in getting you the degree you want. Henry, don't let this become a bigger mess than it already is."

Henry shouted back in great anger and force, "No, you told me that all I had to do was take those stupid college courses, earn a degree, and then I was on my way to a new life. Money, friends, a great apartment, you said it would all be mine. Now it's all fucked up, and we both know it's over. In here, I hear them call me Jen-Lo behind my back or fag and worse. They all hate me. It's bad enough being Mexican and gay in here, but now I'm labeled a cheat and a dummy, all because of that stupid math class that no one was getting."

"If that's true, you all should have said something," Steven sputtered. "For that matter, if you all had flunked the course, that would have blown the whistle on the problem right then and there. He was teaching way over everyone's head. If you had just said something, Henry, we could have dealt with this. Now it's a real mess, I'll grant you that, but I've been here a long time, and I know we can deal with this. We can fix this! Please, just slow down. Calm down. This can be fixed."

"You still don't understand!" yelled Henry. "All I ever wanted was respect. I've sort of had it in here. I was known as a guy who got things done, but now that's all gone. I'll bet my other stuff goes to hell now too. If I'm unemployed in a Shoe unit (special housing unit, where men just out of SEG sat unemployed for ninety days; it was then a new concept at Stillwater, dealing with the many men who were coming in and out of segregation), I won't be able to move around. How am I going to live? My family won't send me money. Fuck! They won't even take my calls, let alone visit. My life is really fucked now!"

Back and forth, they argued all evening. Steve was desperate; he knew how upset Henry was. While Steven knew that he could fix this over time, he also knew how hard it might be to get Henry back in the Spector program.

To Henry, this was the fulfillment of his worst fear, that he would always be an outcast and a looser. "Just another pathetic, looser, gay Mexican," that was his deepest fear.

A DEGREE FOR HENRY

The more he talked and argued with Steven, the more alone and helpless he felt and the angrier he became.

Finally, the count warning bell sounded. Steven headed for the door with a parting thought: "Whatever you do, think this over. We can and we will fix this. Please, Henry, just calm down. We'll start a kite to Pam tomorrow. We can fix this!"

With that thought, he closed Henry's door and went to his own cell for the evening's last count.

At 9:40 PM, the count bell sounded, and C/Os quickly trotted down each of B West's catwalks, pulling on every cell door to ensure that they were locked shut and looking inside to confirm that each cell contained one inmate. About 10:30 PM, the new crew, first watch, made their rounds, shinning a flashlight into each cell to confirm again that each cell was occupied.

With everything in place and all numbers in balance, B West and all of Stillwater settled down for another night.

In his cell, Steven Kline was exhausted. The marathon argument with Henry had really worn him out. On one hand, he felt bad for Henry. This was a real mess, and while Steven was sure he could ultimately repair the damage, it wasn't going to be quick nor easy to repair. As he contemplated the battles to be fought, his fatigue won out, and he fell asleep. This had been an ugly long day.

Two cells to the south, Henry lay on his bunk completely motionless. He knew deep in his soul what this meant, and he knew exactly what he had to do now. He watched as the C/O doing count sped by his cell. Knowing B West's routine, he climbed into bed, after shutting his overhead light off. He lay still, waiting until the 10:30 PM rounds were made and the on-duty C/O flashed the light in his face. Once that C/O was on his/her way, Henry sat up.

With swift, sure movements, Henry stood on the end of his bunk, next to the cell's front side and door, reaching up and over the door casing, where there was an open area about 10 feet high with vertical bars in it matching the patterns of the bars on the door. Quickly and securely, Henry tied the leading edge of his Canteen-purchased, inmate-approved web belt to the middle bar of the set. Giving a firm tug to ensure that it would not slip, he quickly slipped the looped end of the belt over his head, guiding the end tied to the bar to his left side behind his ear. All the while, he was standing as tall as he could to get the loop down where it needed to be, below his chin.

CHARLES SLABAUGH

Taking just a moment for a final thought, Henry mumbled a final "To hell with it!" and he jumped off his bunk.

The knot in the belt did just as Henry had intended. His neck snapped with a popping noise, and he died immediately. His body swung once into the locked cell door, making a loud banging noise, and then quickly came to rest, hanging in midair.

About 10:40 PM, Steven Kline's slumber was interrupted with a loud bang. To Steven, half asleep as he was, the noise sounded like a cell door banging shut. He briefly thought, "Why would anyone's door be closing now?" He lay for another moment and then rolled over and went back to sleep.

The C/O doing rounds at 11:30 PM must have been in a hurry because he/she didn't notice anything amiss when they passed Henry's cell, but the C/O making rounds at 12:30 AM did see Henry hanging just inside the cell door. Quickly keying his radio, he said, "I've got one hanging in B West no. 710, over."

Control acknowledged, asking, "Any sign of life?"

The C/O reached into the cell, through the bars, touching Henry's neck. Finding no pulse, he answered, "No pulse, no movement. No breathing."

"Stand by" came Control's reply.

When the A team arrived in B West and opened cell no. 710, they quickly determined that there was, indeed, no sign of life, and that report was made to Control. With that confirmation, the notification process began. Calls were made to the on-call nurse, the associate warden for operations, the B West lieutenant, the Stillwater chaplain, the warden, and an ambulance was summoned from the town of Stillwater.

The C/O who had made the initial report again asked for direction from Control, "Should we cut him down?"

"Negative" came the reply. "Resume your rounds," and so he did.

As this was occurring, most of B West slept on. Most inmates were used to people walking by their cell door all through the night, and they slept on. The inmates nearby were awakened though, but the staff members responding to the incident ignored them and their questions. "What's going on?"

A DEGREE FOR HENRY

No one was answering any questions. Through it all, Henry's body silently hung in the doorway of cell no. 710.

Stillwater's staff chaplain, a Roman Catholic priest named Sean Gilbertson, had been at the prison for almost eighteen years. An older gentleman with soft eyes and a gentle way, he had long ago arranged to be notified by Control of any inmate or staff death. An officer at Control called Father Gilbertson at 1:22 AM with the report of an inmate's suicide.

Awakening immediately, Father Gilbertson asked who had died and processed the reply. "Henry Jiminez."

Father Gilbertson knew Henry from years of Henry's attending chapel infrequently. Sitting in the back and "doing business" using hushed a voice, Henry had dealt with a wide variety of other inmates. Henry had never exhibited any interest in Bible studies or in any of the regular inmate activities in chapel exhibited by those sincerely interested in worship, but that was unimportant to Father Gilbertson.

Dressing quickly, he drove to the prison and came directly to B West. Confirming that Henry was beyond any earthly assistance, Father Gilbertson went to his office in the chapel and accessed Henry's records in the DOC's computer database. Under emergency notification, Henry's file said, "Earnestine Jiminez" and listed a St. Paul address and phone number.

Without hesitation, Father Gilbertson dialed the number. After several rings, a sleepy voice answered, "Hell-o." Father Gilbertson identified himself and asked if the voice was Ernestine Jiminez. "Yes" came the reply. "Who are you?" Father Gilbertson identified himself, explaining that he was the staff chaplain at Stillwater Prison. With that, Ms. Jiminez gasped, "Is Henry all right?"

Pausing for an instant, Father Gilbertson pressed on explaining why he was calling. "I'm very sorry to inform you that he is dead. If there's . . ."

"No, no!" Ms. Jiminez screamed. "That can't be right. Are you sure you have the right man? You must have made a mistake."

"I'm sorry," the father continued. "There is no mistake. I just came from his cell. It is Henry."

"How did this happen? It just can't be Henry," Mrs. Jiminez continued in a loud voice. "I'm coming to see, I must see for myself."

171

CHARLES SLABAUGH

The father quickly replied, "I'm sorry, but you cannot do that at this time. No one can enter the prison, Ms. Jiminez." He continued, "There will, of course, be an opportunity for you to see him, but not tonight, not in the prison."

"Why? What are you hiding?" Ms. Jiminez shrieked. "What really happened? Who killed my son?"

Swallowing quickly, Father Gilbertson went on, "It appears that Henry took his own life. Ms. Jiminez, I assure you, there will be a thorough and complete investigation. In fact, it is already underway, but I assure you that, at this time, it appears obvious that Henry took his own life. The doctor and those in charge are investigating and will make a complete report of everything. Then an autopsy will be conducted by the medical examiner."

"No, no!" Ms. Jiminez shrieked again. "I do not want Henry's body cut open and ruined. I won't permit that. Henry was my beautiful boy, you can't ruin that too."

"Ms. Jiminez, there is no option. In any death in prison like this one, the law demands an autopsy. You are correct, everything possible will be done to respect Henry and your memory of him. Right now, is there someone I can send to you?"

Ms. Jiminez said, "I'd like to see my daughter, but I don't think that she has a phone . . . Are you sure that Henry is really dead?"

And so the conversation went on for almost thirty minutes. When Father Gilbertson finally got off the phone, he was exhausted and frustrated.

"There ought to be a better way to do this," he mused.

Curious, he again accessed Henry's file in the database and checked the visiting log. Henry's mother was on his list of approved visitors, and she had last visited him seven years before. Henry's sister was not an approved visitor. In fact, Ms. Jiminez was Henry's only approved visitor. Under religious preferences, Henry had listed "Zen." With that, Father Gilbertson sighed and made a short prayer for Henry's soul and then another prayer for his mother. Then Father Gilbertson returned to B West.

By then, the prison's doctor, Dr. Blumenthal, had been there, confirmed the death, and had already left. An ambulance crew was standing by to remove the body to the Ramsey County medical examiner's suite for an autopsy. Stillwater's associate warden for operations was now in B West. Through it all, most of B West slept on, and Henry hung in the doorway of cell no. 710.

A DEGREE FOR HENRY

With dawn approaching, the associate warden for operations was concerned that the scene needed to be cleaned up before the movement for breakfast began at 6:40 AM. With that in mind, the belt holding Henry's body was cut. Henry's body smashed into the concrete floor with a resounding smack. The ambulance crew quickly loaded him onto a gurney and started down B West's main staircase across the flag and then outside to their ambulance.

Control received three incoming calls from Ernestine Jiminez during the morning, demanding to speak with Chaplain Gilbertson. When advised that he had left the building, she demanded his home number. Advised that it was unavailable, Ms. Jiminez said that she was coming to Stillwater to "clear this mistake up! This is just stupid." Ms. Jiminez yelled into the phone, "My Henry is such a good boy. He'd never kill himself."

Control told her that she could not enter Stillwater that night and referred her to the warden's office, which they advised her would be open for business after 8:30 AM. When she called the warden's office later that morning, she was referred to the Ramsey County medical examiner's office.

Inside B West, cell no. 710 was taped over with yellow tape, proclaiming it a crime scene, and things began to return to normal. When Steven Kline left his cell, cell no. 712, on his way to breakfast, the yellow tape on his friend's door told him that there had been trouble but little else. One his way out of B West, he asked the C/O at the door what had happened. The C/O would only say "I can't say."

At breakfast, there were many rumors and much speculation, but no one seemed sure what had happened. Returning from breakfast, Steven saw the B West lieutenant and detoured to him to ask about his friend. "He's gone. He hung himself last night" was the answer.

Steven was so upset, he almost lost his breakfast on the spot.

In the aftermath of Henry's death, Steven learned that twenty-four members of the class Math for Liberal Arts had been caught cheating. Someone, no one knew who for sure, had stolen a copy of the instructor's answer sheet for the midterm exam. What they did not know was that they had the alternate copy of the test. All the answers were wrong for the test that was actually administered. They were caught because each man turned in identical wrong answers. They had all memorized well.

Two months later, the Stillwater *The Prison Mirror* published a short article about Henry, mentioning his determination to get ahead in life.

CHARLES SLABAUGH

About the same time, Steven Kline finally got to the hospital to have his acid reflux problems checked out. The minute the doctors saw the live images on the screen, they knew the answer: esophageal cancer. Steven was dead within the year at the Oak Park Heights supermax's infirmary.

Index

A

American Corrections Association, 46
anthropology, 56, 58, 62, 67, 71
Appleton, 91
Armstrong, Donte, vii, 32–36
assault, 90, 103–4, 111, 116

B

Bert (Bernard's aunt), 83–84
Bible, 20, 124, 126, 159–60, 171
Bishop, Dale, vii, 43–45, 55, 104–5, 112, 144–46, 148–49, 160
bit, 62, 74, 76, 97–98
Blumenthal, Orland, vii, 56, 63, 70, 73, 139, 172

C

California, 91, 150–53, 155, 157
Canteen, x, 18, 21, 25–26, 29, 53, 62, 84–85, 88, 105, 108, 118
case worker, 6, 82, 115, 136
CD (chemical dependency), 98
chapel, 20, 43–44, 46, 50, 55, 65, 70, 82, 117, 121, 126, 137–40, 147–48, 158–60, 171
Chicago, 77–78, 88, 99
cho-mos, ix, 74–75, 101–2, 110
Christian, 45, 55, 86, 137

C/O (correction officer), ix, 2–5, 8–12, 17, 19–20, 22, 24, 27–29, 34–35, 37, 49, 59, 61, 69–70, 81, 98, 103, 109–10, 112–13, 116, 125, 138, 140, 155–56, 160, 169–70, 173
Colchran, Bob, vii, 25, 31–32, 35–36
Colson, Charles, 5
contraband, ix, 43, 51
controlled movement, ix, 14–15, 19, 43, 50, 55, 140, 145, 158, 162
convictions, 66, 90
Correction Officers' Union, 46

D

Dassel, Pauly, vii, 86–88, 97–98
degree
  AA, 53, 158
  college, 52–53, 56–57, 62, 64, 71–72, 74, 160, 163, 167
Dent, Samuel, vii, 101–2, 109–11, 116
Diamond, Bernard, vii, 77–90, 94–100
Diamond, Jerome, 81–82
diploma, 37–39, 47–48, 59–60, 132
discipline system, 41, 112, 118
DOC (Department of Corrections), ix, 2, 12, 19, 26, 39, 41, 47–48, 54, 58–59, 84, 116, 119, 121, 132
Dombroski, Shirley, vii, 164
double-bunking, 46

E

Eckonalanza, Soma, vii, 134
education, viii, x, 17, 36, 50–52, 54, 62, 102, 150, 155, 157
Education Building, 64, 69, 107, 143, 163, 168
Education Department, 45, 59, 61, 66, 74, 117, 125, 143, 151
Encarta Encyclopedia, 86–87, 96
English, 37–39, 47–48, 56, 68, 92–93, 105–7, 116, 164
ESL (English as a second language), 37–38, 164

F

Faribault, x, 90–91, 95–97, 100, 144–45, 148
Folsom Prison, 152, 159

G

gangs, 92, 94, 102, 111, 121–22
Garza, Raphael, vii, 90–92, 94
GED diploma, 37, 39, 48, 53, 58, 132–33
GED exams, 48, 61–62, 78, 118, 134–36
Gilbertson, Sean, vii, 82–84, 137, 139–41, 171–73
God's Truth Church, 84
Goodwin, Doris Kerns, 5
Granite City, 2
Gravenhorst, Cecil, vii, 114–15, 127–36
Gravenhorst, Geri, 127–31, 136
Gravenhorst, Sara, 127–31, 136
Great Lakes, 78

H

Halverson, Jane, vii, 38–39, 46–48, 58–61, 66, 68–69, 74, 77–78, 80–82, 86–95, 97–99, 104–7, 114, 133–34, 136, 162–63, 165
Hmong, 68, 78, 106–7, 120

I

Iron Range, 127, 132
Islam, 86–88, 125

J

Jacobs, Arturo, vii, 38–39
Jergens, Donald, vii, 62, 162–65
Jesse James Gang, 45
Jiminez, Ernestine, vii, 171–73
Jiminez, Henry, vii, 39–41, 43, 49–58, 62–67, 69–76, 101, 105–7, 110–11, 114, 116, 167–73
jobs, ix, 7, 11–12, 14–19, 23, 25–27, 32–33, 36, 38–39, 47–49, 51–53, 58, 61, 70, 72, 81, 108, 115, 118–19, 121–24, 130, 133, 138, 143, 151, 157
Johns, Ned, vii, 117–19, 145

K

kite, 82–83, 89, 118, 135, 158, 163, 169
Kline, Steven, vii, 38–39, 49, 52–58, 62–67, 69–76, 101, 105–6, 110–11, 114–16, 129–32, 136, 167–70, 173–74
Kolkins, Norma, vii, 54, 56, 72, 164–65

L

Latin Kings, 90, 92, 94
Lee, Shoua, vii, 68–69, 73–74, 106–7
lifer, vii, 33, 117, 140, 145
Lindberg, Charles, 96
literacy classes, 37, 62, 78
literacy program, 101, 132

M

Marcus, Stanley, vii, 94, 158, 163
Maud (Sara's sister), 129–31, 136
Max (inmate), 144–49
MCF
    Faribault, 90, 100, 144–45, 148
    Oak Park Heights, 100

Red Wing, 91
St. Cloud, 1–7, 9, 11, 14, 16–17, 46, 51, 66, 78, 122
Stillwater, 9–10, 12, 15, 17, 29, 45, 123
Minncor Industries, x, 3, 12, 17, 29, 32, 35–36, 84, 108, 125, 138
Minnesota, x, 1, 8–9, 18, 36, 45, 90–91, 104, 151, 153–54, 156–57, 164
Minnesota Department of Corrections, 1, 3, 56, 84, 123
Minnesota Legislature, 3, 46–47, 84
Minnesota literacy council, 92–94
Minnesota State Prison, 1
Mohammed, Elijah, 86–87

N

National Adult Honor Society, 59–62
Natives, 50, 53, 121

O

Oak Park Heights, 13, 22, 41, 98, 100, 139, 141, 148, 174
offenders, x, 11, 19, 60, 70, 81, 99–100, 118
OIC (officer in charge), 166
Oogolala, Omar, vii, 46–48, 58–62, 104–6, 112, 134, 145, 162
Osborne, Nathan, vii, 101–4

P

parole, x, 2, 33, 81, 108, 150, 156–60
Pawlenty (governor), 45–46
phonics, 47–48, 80, 86, 106–7
PMB (Prison Motor Bike Gang), 65, 101–2, 151, 158–59
Polinski, Pamela, viii, 54–55, 60–61, 119, 163–64, 167–69
Prison Fellowship, 5
Prison Mirror, 45, 55, 61, 104, 173
prison system, ix, 38, 45, 90, 150, 157
Property Department, 11, 13–15, 70, 108, 125, 154
Protestantism, 137

R

Ramsey County, 172–73
Rasmusson, Paul, viii, 150–61
Red Wing, x, 91
religions, 125, 158–59
Roman Catholic, vii, 39, 55, 70, 83, 137, 146, 171
Roosevelt, Franklin, 87–88
Rush City, 6

S

security, 10, 24, 35, 61, 68, 70, 121, 139
SEG (segregation unit), x, 22–25, 35, 37, 41–43, 49, 53, 55, 65, 68–69, 91, 94, 104, 111, 113–15, 118, 133, 136, 138, 168
sentence
  life without parole, 33, 45, 47, 132, 150, 159
  segregation, 23, 152–53
shakedown, 20, 59, 61, 112–14
Shepherd (inmate), 31–32
Simonton, Ben, viii, 137–42
SO (sexual offender), x, 74, 123
Sorenson, Dale, 109, 116
Sorenson, Douglas, viii, 74–76, 101–4, 109–10, 112–13, 116
Southern Minnesota, 1, 144, 157
Spanish, 39, 92–93
Spector program, vii, x, 52–55, 63, 69, 165, 167–68
St. Cloud Prison, 1–7, 9, 11, 14, 16–19, 31, 46, 51, 75, 78, 91–92, 122
Stillwater, ix–x, 8–10, 12–21, 23–27, 29, 31, 34–35, 40–41, 44–47, 49–50, 61, 68, 70–71, 73–74, 76, 98–99, 101–3, 114–17, 120–21, 132–33, 136–39, 141–44, 146, 148, 151, 158–59, 162–63, 165, 168–70, 172–73
Stillwater Prison, 10–11, 40, 45, 57, 115, 119, 132, 156, 171
Stillwater Territorial Prison, 45

177

St. Paul, 2, 40, 60–61, 104, 121, 171
suicide, 171
Sullivan, Harold, viii, 133–35
swamper, viii, 21, 28, 38, 49–51, 122–23, 125, 148

T

Tofte, Owen, viii, 122–26
Transitions Department, 119
TU (temporarily unemployed inmate), 14, 25
tutors, vii–viii, 36, 38–39, 49–52, 57, 59–60, 62, 66, 69–70, 74, 85, 87, 95, 97–99, 107, 116, 133–34, 136, 162
Twin Cities, 2, 26, 80, 158

U

UA (urine analysis), x, 151
UI (unemployed inmate), 92, 124, 138, 152
US Army, 2–3, 19, 120

V

Ventura (governor), 45

W

Warren, Robert, viii, 17–18
Wilson (case worker), 6–7

Z

Zantac, 56–57, 63, 70, 73, 114, 116

Made in the USA
Monee, IL
03 January 2025